101
Ideas for

Homebrew
Fun

Ray Daniels

Brewers Publications
Boulder, Colorado

Brewers Publications, Division of the Association of Brewers
PO Box 1679, Boulder, CO 80306-1679
(303) 447-0816; Fax (303) 447-2825

Printed in the United States of America
10 9 8 7 6 5 4 3 2 1

ISBN 0-937381-57-8

Library of Congress Cataloging-in-Publication Data
Daniels, Ray.
    101 ideas for homebrew fun / by Ray Daniels.
        p.   cm.
    Includes index.
    ISBN 0-937381-57-8 (alk. paper)
    1. Brewing—Amateurs' manuals. I. Title.
TP570.D36   1998
663' .3—dc21   97-47350
                                                  CIP

Please direct all inquiries or orders to the above address.

Give a man a beer, and he wastes an hour;
Teach a man to brew, and he wastes a lifetime.
—*Motto of the St. Louis Brews homebrew club*

This book is dedicated to the Chicago Beer Society and to all homebrew clubs where fun, fellowship, and fine beer bring brewers together.

CONTENTS

1 Hobgoblin's Great Pumpkin Beer 5

2 Something for Everyone: A Crystal Malt Tasting 7

3 A Gin-Dandy Idea 9

4 Have Glass, Will Travel 11

5 A Wonderful Wheat Beer Is within Your Reach 13

6 Longing to Lauter: A Simple Start 15

7 Home-Toasted Malt Gives Flavor and Complexity 18

8 Hard Cider That's a Snap 20

9 The Breakfast (Cereal) of Champions 22

10 Mead from Heaven 23

11 A Rye Refresher 25

12 Just a Spoon Full of Malt . . . 27

13 Caramel Malt Bread 28

14 Malt Extract Bread 31

15 Spent Grain Cookies 32

16 Hop Coffee Gets Your Morning Going 33

17 Rest Easy on a Pillow of Hops 34

18 Stump the Experts 35

19 Hold a Weizen Beer Brunch 36

20 Start a Six-Pack Club 38

21 Brew in the Zoo (and Other Wacky Places) 39

22 Brew Up Root Beer for the Kids or Yourself! 41

23 Barbecue Your Malt for That Tangy, Smoked-Beer Flavor 43

24	Thinking Small: Test Batch Brewing	45
25	Yeast: It Takes All Types	46
26	Beat That! Brewoffs Level the Playing Field	48
27	Flavor Encounter: Eau de Skunk	49
28	Malt Waffles	52
29	Half-Wit Chicken	53
30	Check Your Sanity	54
31	You Will See Clearly Now . . .	56
32	In the Temperate Zone	57
33	Dial-a-Homebrew Project	58
34	Judges' Corner	61
35	Challenge Your Taste Buds	62
36	Toss Some Rocks in Your Beer	63
37	Pass the Milk: A Malt Tasting	64
38	A Jolly Ale for Old Saint Nick	66
39	Malt Extract Evaluation	68
40	Mix Up Your Own Beer Cocktails	70
41	Cock Ale if You Dare	72
42	Lob Some Fruit into Your Beer	73
43	Honey of a Beer	76
44	Infect Your Beer for Classic Belgian Flavor	78
45	A Religious Experience with Belgian Ale	80
46	Time for a Yeast Safari	82
47	Are You Porter or Stout?	84

48	Take a Cool Sip of Your Warm Beer	86
49	The Beer Rainbow, or, What Color Is Your Beer?	88
50	Wood Aging Your Beer	90
51	Break Your Vacuum	92
52	Dry Hop with Chili Peppers	93
53	Special Spiked Ale the Easy Way	94
54	Progressive Beer Dinner	95
55	Make a Name for Your Beer	96
56	Grow Your Own Hops	98
57	Consort with the Devil: Hold a Hop Festival	100
58	Have a Meeting with Style	101
59	Brew in the Woods	102
60	Stunted Growth: The Magic of Malt	104
61	Bring Your Buddies to a Brew-a-thon	106
62	Sour Mash Beer	107
63	Caramelize Your Wort for Special Flavor	111
64	A Pale Imitator	112
65	Have Beer, Will Travel	114
66	Here's Air in Your Beer	115
67	A Cozy Keg Is a Cool Keg	116
68	Welcome Life with Majority Ale	117
69	Cure the Bitterness Blues	119
70	Build Your Own Multitap Dispenser	121
71	Hold a Honey Tasting	124

72	Vulgare Day	126
73	World's Longest Beer Run	128
74	This Beer Will Cook Your Goose	129
75	Send Your Beer on a Cruise	130
76	Here's a Cool Fermentation Idea	132
77	Forget about Your Beer to Improve Its Flavor	135
78	A Soft Spot for Pretzels	136
79	Big Bad Barley Wine	138
80	Make Your Own Cask Ale	140
81	Hold a Homebrew Expo	141
82	Speed Your Grain Drain	143
83	Travel through Time with Beer	144
84	Smokin' Good Chili	145
85	Spice and Easy	146
86	Smoked Porter Cheesecake	147
87	911 for Brewers	150
88	Tasting Treats	151
89	Fill Your Tankard with Lambswool	152
90	Bappir Brew	153
91	Celebrate a Wedding with Bride Ale	156
92	Spruce Up Your Beer	158
93	Vanilla Malt Freeze	160
94	Plan a Brewer's Tour of Europe	161
95	Adorn Yourself with Beer	164

96	Beer Repair	165
97	Drop-by-Drop Beer Chronicle	166
98	Make Your Own Malt Vinegar	167
99	Carrot Beer	168
100	Hop Jelly	170
101	Orange Ambrosia Mead	171

Glossary 175

References 179

Index 180

Homebrew Bloopers

It's a Geyser! 8

Energetic Brewing 12

It's the Pits! 19

Impure as the Driven Snow 44

A Shattering Experience 69

One Determined Brewer 87

Dryer Hopping 91

Lion, Tigers, and Bugs! 148

Quick Carbonation—Not! 162

Guest Profiles

Tom Klopfer—Burning Desire to Brew 16

Pete Slosberg—From Homebrew to National Brand 29

Randy Mosher—Creative Force 50

xi

Chuck Skypeck—Home Innovation Drives
    Commercial Success   59
Bill Owens—Industry Pioneer   74
Jim Parker—This Is Fun!   109
Darryl Richman—Keep It Simple   122
Tim and Dot Artz—Still Brewin' after All These Years   133
Maribeth "MB" Raines and Steve Casselman—
    A Match Made in Maltose   172

INTRODUCTION

IN THE SUMMER OF 1989, I was waiting for my order at a tiny hamburger joint near my home in Chicago when I happened across an ad for a nearby homebrew supply store. I'd heard one or two friends talk about homebrewing, and it sounded interesting. Now I knew where I could check it out.

A week later, I visited that homebrew store with a buddy, Gary Gerdemann. Although puzzled by the different style designations on the kits, we picked out ingredients for a couple of batches, along with a basic equipment package and a book. The next day we brewed. When that first beer was ready to drink, we pronounced it good. Even our friends drank it without protest. Emboldened by our success, we moved on to batch two and, not long after that, batch three.

Had we not brewed batch three before batch two was ready, you might not be reading this today. Batch two was a stinker: an unmitigated, massively infected failure. Only one of our friends, a fellow named Brian Davis, would drink it.

Batch three was a different story. An India pale ale, it included freshly toasted malt and other grains in addition to liberally applied flavor and aroma hops. To my memory, batch three was nectar from heaven. We thought it was better than anything we'd ever drunk from tap or bottle anywhere in the world. Not surprisingly, it quickly disappeared.

After batch three, I knew "homebrewer" would be a part of my identity for a long time to come. There was no looking back.

Today, as I bear down on batch 200, I can reflect on all the fun I've had through homebrewing. Indeed, the purpose of this book is to share some of that fun with you.

You can harvest the fun of homebrewing in many different ways. Of course brewing beer is one of those, and this book includes a collection of fun recipes I've made through the years. If you've ever wanted to experiment with mead, cider, *kvass*, or vegetables in your brewing, you'll find a few treasures in the pages that follow. But, there's more than just recipes here.

When I first started brewing, I was fanatical and brewed nearly every weekend. Monday through Friday I thought about brewing, read about brewing, and, of course, enjoyed the fruits of my labor. On week nights when I couldn't actually brew, I found other projects to keep me busy—building equipment, tasting beers, exploring resources. If you find your appetite for brewing unleashed at odd moments, you'll find amongst the pages to come many ideas that can be tackled in an hour of free time or less.

After a few months of brewing, I learned about a nearby homebrew group. Curious whether the snobbery of wine lovers had spilled over into beer, I saddled up and headed out to my first meeting of the Chicago Beer Society. The folks I met at that meeting welcomed me (and my homebrew!) with open arms and open attitudes. The club is the most collegial gathering of people I've ever enjoyed.

Soon I was helping to organize the talents and resources of this group. Before long we had two homebrew club meetings each month and a couple of annual brew-ins. At one point, more than 100 people were showing up for our monthly meetings at the Goose Island brewpub. We weren't fanatical about winning awards or electing officers—we just liked to have good homebrew fun. Many, many great ideas came out of the group, and we did a heck of a lot of them.

I've learned that much of what is fun about homebrew involves groups of people. Whether it's just you and a friend or a group of several dozen, companionship enhances much of homebrewing. Each person has a different perspective, a different set of skills, a different set of taste buds. Individually you can learn a lot, and collectively, you can learn a lot more and have a lot of fun.

For this reason, some of the activities that follow are for groups. Many home-brewers already belong to a club; others may be looking for a reason to join one or form one in their area. I hope these group-related activities will provide an impetus for such socialization, even if it's only temporary.

Brewers of all levels can enjoy this book. In fact, the more recently you have taken up the hobby, the greater the ideas you're likely to find here. Still, veterans can find plenty of new riffs: new recipes to try, new tastes to explore, new ways to have fun with homebrew.

In the pages that follow, I hope to help all homebrewers do more than just make and drink homebrew. I hope to introduce you to new ways to have fun with this hobby while learning more about beer, brewing, and our fellow brewers around the world.

1

HOBGOBLIN'S GREAT PUMPKIN BEER

WHEN FALL IS IN THE AIR, a brewer's thoughts often turn to pumpkins—and how they might be used in beer. Several tasty and delightful beers can be made using the pumpkin theme. Some recipes rely only on pumpkin pie spices, but this one also uses real pumpkins. Here's the drill:

PUMPKIN BEER (makes 5 gallons)
2 fresh pumpkins, each 8–10 inches in diameter (You can substitute two 15-ounce cans of pumpkin instead, but it won't taste as good!)
1 teaspoon pumpkin pie spice (optional)
2 pounds two-row or pale ale malt (ground)
0.5 pound light-colored Crystal or caramel malt
5 pounds light dry malt extract or two 3.3-pound cans of liquid light extract (All-grain brewers can use 9 additional pounds of two-row or pale ale malt instead of the extract.)
0.75 ounce Cascade hops
1 ounce flavor hops (Hallertau, Tettnang, Saaz, Mt. Hood, or Crystal)
Ale yeast

You'll also need a brewpot, a thermometer (optional), and a large strainer (or lauter tun for 3 pounds of grain). Clean the seeds and stringy stuff out of the pumpkins as if making jack-o-lanterns; then cut the pumpkins into pieces for baking. Bake on cookie sheets at 325 °F (163 °C) for 1.5 to 2 hours or until soft. Puree the pumpkin in a food processor or blender.

All-grain brewers should add the pumpkin to your mash and hold at about 150 °F (65 °C). From here, follow your regular sparge and boil procedures.

Extract brewers should add the canned or pureed pumpkin along with the crushed grains to 3 quarts of your hottest tap water. Mix thoroughly. Ideally, this mixture should be held between 145 and 155 °F (63 and 68 °C) for about an hour. (If you don't have thermometer, just make sure it stays too hot to put your finger in but doesn't start steaming.)

After steeping the grains and pumpkin, lauter this mixture or remove the grain using a strainer. Use about a gallon of very hot water (170 °F [77 °C]) to sparge in the lauter tun, or rinse the grains in the strainer. If the strainer doesn't hold all the grains at once, split up the rinse water so all grains are well rinsed.

Next, add the malt extract and the Cascade hops to this wort. Also, add enough water to fill your brewpot. Bring this mixture to a boil. After boiling for 30 minutes, add 1/2 ounce of flavor hops. Boil another 20 minutes and add the remaining flavor hops. After another 10 minutes, turn off the fire. Chill and ferment this wort following your normal procedures.

If you want to make a beer that tastes like pumpkin pie rather than having just a hint of pumpkin, add the teaspoon of pumpkin pie spice about 5 minutes before the end of the boil. (If you forget, just add it while the beer is cooling.)

The finished beer should have a subtle pumpkin flavor and a pale orange hue—the perfect beer for your Thanksgiving or holiday feast!

SOMETHING FOR EVERYONE: A CRYSTAL MALT TASTING

EVEN IF YOU'RE NOT AN ALL-GRAIN BREWER, you can greatly influence your beer with the specific types of specialty grains you select. At this point, you may think one Crystal or caramel malt is pretty much the same as the next. In truth, these products vary considerably. Taste a few of the malts described below, and you'll enjoy using this specialty malt even more. Plus, you'll find you can change the flavor of beer you brew just by changing the type of Crystal malt you use.

Crystal or caramel malt was invented around 1875. It's made by a special process called "stewing," which mimics mashing and converts the starch inside the whole malt kernel to sugar. Afterward the kernel is dried and toasted, causing the sugar to caramelize and crystallize inside.

Most maltsters make a few different grades of Crystal malt. They are designated by a color rating according to the Lovibond system. These Lovibond numbers range from a low of about 10 to a high of about 120 °L for Crystal malt. At each color increment, the flavor of the malt changes slightly.

In addition to the variations produced by each maltster, there are differences between maltsters. Every maltster conducts the caramelization process a bit differently. As a result, the flavors of one maltster's 50 °L Crystal will vary from those of another maltster's 50 °L Crystal. To better appreciate these differences, try sampling a few different types. Here's what I recommend.

Find one maltster that makes three distinct grades of Crystal malt. Try to get one in the 10 to 35 °L range, one in the 40 to 70 °L range, and one in the 80 °L or higher range. Notice the flavor differences among them as the color rating changes. At the same time, try to determine the "family" flavor—the components that remain the same from sample to sample.

After this, you're ready to compare Crystal malts made by other maltsters. Try to match the Lovibond rating of the middle malt just mentioned from two other sources. If possible, get a mix of malts from different countries, including Germany, Belgium, Britain, and the United States.

You can do this alone, with a small group, or as part of a large homebrew gathering. It's fun and educational in any setting. And if you record your impressions of each malt sample, they'll come in handy next time you're trying to decide which malt to buy for a recipe.

It's a Geyser! The first time Larry used whole hops, the brew turned out normal in most respects. After chilling, he filled his glass carboy up to the neck with wort, pitched the yeast, and slapped on a carboy cap with his usual blowoff tube. A day later, fermentation was in full swing inside the fermenter, but he wasn't getting much blowoff into the sanitizer. Things seemed fine though, so he decided not to worry.

Early the next day, Larry heard a loud pop. He turned toward his fermenter just in time to see a geyser of beer hit the ceiling and watched as half the contents of the carboy began to splatter all around the room. A minute later, standing in a beer-doused room, Larry inspected the carboy cap. The whole hop cones from the brew had become lodged in the entrance to the blowoff tube, effectively sealing it. Pressure had built up steadily inside the carboy until the cap blew off, creating a geyser of beer.

The next time Larry brewed, he made sure to remove the whole hops before he put the wort into the fermenter. He also made sure to leave plenty of headspace in the fermenter the next time he made a beer using whole fruit in the fermenter.

A year later, he was still trying to get the beer stains and yeast smell out of the carpet.

A GIN-DANDY IDEA

IN SOUTHERN FINLAND, a special brew called *sahti* is made from malted barley and rye. Juniper used during brewing contributes a distinct flavor to the finished product—the same flavor found in Dutch gin.

Juniper was originally used by brewers to help separate the wort from the mash. They placed a mesh of branches at the bottom of the mash tun and across the drain hole. This held back husks and grain bits while allowing the liquid to drain. Because the branches were not stripped of their berries and needles, they contributed flavor to the brew.

In 1994, Mike Schaefer of Milwaukee's Brewtown Brewmasters homebrew club researched the subject of sahti for an article in *Zymurgy*® magazine. The recipes he listed included malted rye or rye flour for 5 to 25 percent of the grain bill. Juniper was added as either berries or branches during the brewing process. Most of the recipes also included some hops.

The type of juniper to use is *Juniperus communis,* or common juniper. It is a small shrub, four to six feet high, widely distributed throughout the Northern Hemisphere. The berries are well known as a flavoring agent, and herbalists recommend them for their diuretic properties. (Pregnant women and people with kidney problems should take a pass on juniper beers!)

You can sometimes find juniper berries at your local homebrew store or through homebrew mail-order outfits. You also might check the health food or herbal medicine shop. If you're botanically inclined, just collect some boughs and branches from a local tree!

Because rye extract can't be had, you'll have to use some grain to make this brew—but it needn't be a big production. Here's my recipe:

SIMPLE SAHTI (makes 3 gallons)
1 pound flaked rye or crushed, malted rye
1 pound crushed two-row Pilsener or pale ale malt
1 can light or pale malt extract syrup, your choice of brand
0.5 ounce Cascade hop pellets
1 ounce crushed, dried juniper berries
Ale yeast

Combine the rye flakes and crushed malt in a large grain bag. Put them in 1.5 gallons of cold water in a pot on the stove. Turn on the heat to medium. Stir the grain bag every 5 to 10 minutes. When the water starts to boil, turn off the heat and remove the grain bag, leaving behind as much liquid from the grains as possible. (A good pair of rubber gloves can be handy here.) Now add the malt extract and hops and, if your pot will hold it, another 1.5 gallons of water.

Turn on the heat, bring this wort to a boil, and boil for 45 minutes. Then turn off the heat and add an ounce of crushed, dried juniper berries. Let it stand 15 minutes and then chill. Transfer the chilled wort to the fermenter, and add cold water to bring the total volume to about 3 gallons. Mix and pitch with ale yeast.

When the sahti is finished (no pun intended), you'll have the perfect refresher for your next trip to the sauna!

4

HAVE GLASS, WILL TRAVEL

WHEN HOMEBREW IS BEING POURED at a party or an event, it's easy to lose your glass. Usually the glasses all look the same. The minute you put yours down (and at some point, you just have to!), it gets mixed up with another one or simply forgotten. Until you find a new glass, you go thirsty.

Beer geeks all over the world have suffered from this problem, and some have come up with innovative solutions. Here are two I've seen.

THE NECK GLASS

A few years back, Chicago's Tim Norris organized the "crazy train," a rail car dedicated to carrying homebrewers to the National Homebrewers Conference. Copious quantities of homebrew were consumed along the way, of course, and Tim solved the lost (and spilled) glass problem with the neck glass. It's a plastic glass that some describe as a thistle and which I think looks like the pointy top of some medieval church tower. The pointy end is down, so the glass can't be set down when there's beer in it. Instead, the glass is fitted with a neck lanyard that allows the user to wear the glass around his or her neck. With the glass (and beer) safely nestled against the user's chest, he or she always knows where the glass is, empty or full. Crazy train passengers decorated and customized their glasses along the way so each one had a distinct personality when the trip was done.

Security is knowing where your beer glass is

THE GLASS HOLSTER

Brewer Tim Rastetter found another innovative solution to this problem: a small holster attached to his belt that securely held a tall, thin *kölsch*-style glass. (Randy Mosher dubbed it the "kölschter.") Tim had hastily fashioned his out of duct tape, but someone with a bit of leather-working knowledge could make a classy little number for everyone in the club. Personally, I'd wear one to all those beer festivals where there's no place to set down your beer!

Energetic Brewing   A brewing consultant was called in to troubleshoot at a relatively new brewery. The owner was not highly experienced in brewing, but he assured the consultant he was an engineer and was "well read" on the subject. The consultant tasted the beers, and they were awful—massively infected, full of protein haze, and decidedly lacking in most identifiable beer flavors.

The consultant started his tour of the brewery in the areas that seemed most likely to harbor the culprit: first the packaging section, then the fermenters, then the yeast-handling equipment. He saw some things that could be improved, but nothing struck him as being so terribly wrong it could produce the beers he had tasted.

At first, the brewhouse also seemed normal: the mash/lauter tun and boiling kettle looked like any other from the outside. He looked inside and was struck by the curious design of the kettle. Instead of a steam coil or jacket, he found a set of mixing paddles.

"What are these for?" he asked the owner.

"This is how we apply energy to the wort in the kettle," the owner answered. "By turning the paddles at high speed, we apply enough energy to equal that of a steam coil. It's more efficient, and it's faster than boiling. Clever, don't you think?"

His engineering mind-set had caused the owner to overlook some of the roles boiling plays in beer production—things like sanitizing the wort, extracting hop bitterness, and coagulating proteins. Needless to say, the consultant recommended a redesign of the kettle so each wort received a proper ninety-minute boil. The beers improved immeasurably.

5

A WONDERFUL WHEAT
BEER IS WITHIN YOUR REACH

HOMEBREW STORE OWNERS SAY customers often ask for an easy way to make a wheat beer. Some want an American-style wheat ale like the Widmer Hefeweizen. Others desire the traditional German-style *weizen* with a distinct banana-and-clove character—something like Schneider Weisse or Paulaner Hefeweizen.

Like many others, I too love a great German weizen beer. But as a beginning homebrewer, I was frustrated by the failure of my early attempts to replicate the flavor of store-bought examples I had tried. Eventually, I found out the secret was in the yeast. I played around a bit with different approaches and learned that as long as the yeast is right, most everything else will be okay.

Does that mean you can make a great wheat beer using extract? You bet it does! Three pounds of grain plus a can of extract will produce a really nice weizen beer in either the German or American style. The only difference between the two types is in—you guessed it—the yeast.

For an American-style wheat beer, nearly any dry yeast or liquid American ale or Chico ale yeast can be used. For a German weizen, choose a proper weizen yeast. Examples of this are often labeled as "Weihenstephen" weizen yeast. The Wyeast (number 3068) example is readily available, and I've also had good experience with the strain available from Yeast Labs (W51). Other sources can supply similar yeast strains.

For the best results with a true weizen strain, ferment at temperatures less than 70 °F (21 °C), preferably between 60 and 65 °F (15 and 18 °C). Don't sweat it if you can't achieve this the first time, but keep it in mind as a goal.

This recipe calls for "wheat extract." Most products with this label are a blend of barley and wheat malt extracts in which wheat accounts for 40 to 60 percent of the content. This is the standard ratio of wheat to barley in wheat beer recipes, so this type of product is perfect for this recipe.

WONDERFUL WEIZEN (makes 3 gallons)
Target original gravity: 1.052
2 pounds wheat malt
1 pound Pilsener or two-row malt
2.25 pounds wheat extract (see note above)
0.375 ounce Perle hops (about 3 alpha-acid units)

Mini-mash the crushed grains or soak them in 2 to 3 gallons of water at 150 °F (65 °C) for about an hour. Then remove the grains with a strainer or grain bag. Add the extract, hops, and enough water to equal 3.5 gallons or the capacity of your brewpot. Boil for 60 to 75 minutes. Chill and pitch with yeast.

When this beer is done, consider matching it with the foods mentioned in Idea 19: Hold a Weizen Beer Brunch.

6

LONGING TO LAUTER: A SIMPLE START

ALL-GRAIN BREWING is the extreme approach to homebrewing. It takes time. It takes money. It takes work. But for some in the homebrewing community, it's the only way to go. Other brewers are happy with their grain-and-extract brews, but they'd like to be able to mash a small quantity of grain without committing half the kitchen and a week's pay to the equipment.

Regardless of which camp you belong to, if you don't have a way to mash and lauter five pounds of grain or less, this project is for you. You can create and assemble this small-volume mash/lauter tun in an evening and use it for years.

This masher consists of two elements. To help hold the mash at a steady temperature, use an insulated plastic two-gallon cylindrical picnic cooler. (It should have a removable top and a spigot on the side near the bottom.) In a vessel this size, you can mash up to about five pounds of grain.

Inside the cooler, the second element—a small collapsible vegetable steamer—forms a false bottom for lautering. The kind of vegetable steamer I'm talking about has a bunch of hinged plates around the outside and opens up like a flower. This feature provides a good fit around the edge in containers of different sizes.

In some cases, at least, you can use these items right off the shelf to perform a successful mash. But I found that modifying the cooler's spigot was well worthwhile for my own system. The main thing is to have a spigot you can open and leave open without having to stand there and hold it. Also, remember that pieces of husk and grain will get past the false bottom. You'll have less trouble with clogging if the spigot opening is at least three-sixteenths of an inch wide.

In my system, I completely removed the spring-type spigot that came on the cooler by unscrewing it from the inside. I replaced it with a simple hose barb, but other types of spigots are often sold in homebrew stores. Or check out the hardware store, surplus supply houses, and plastic supply catalogs for options.

Once you've got your system together, you're ready to mash. First time out, limit the amount you mash to no more than three pounds. Also, be gentle when stirring so you don't tip the vegetable steamer. With just a little care, you should have no problems.

For directions on mashing, consult your favorite brewing book. Mash away!

Tom Klopfer—Burning Desire to Brew

Based in Anchorage, Alaska, Tom Klopfer is a relatively recent convert to homebrewing. But like many others before him, he's gotten a serious case of the homebrew bug.

As a battalion chief in the Anchorage Fire Department, he works twenty-four-hour shifts. "I have a lot of time to read about brewing and plan my next beer," he says. "Plus, every other day, I'm at home where I can brew."

In just two-and-a-half years of brewing, Klopfer completed nearly seventy batches of beer and accumulated a vast collection of homebrew gear—including a custom-made stainless-steel all-grain system and more than twenty soda kegs.

"In a lot of ways, Alaska is a perfect place to be a homebrewer," he says. "Because of our weather, the brewing season starts earlier and lasts longer—and when we need something chilled, we just set it out on the patio."

The Anchorage economy also offers unique advantages to brewers. Surplus oil-field gear can often be acquired inexpensively, and a good deal of it has been incorporated into Klopfer's custom-made mash/lauter tun. When it comes to getting all the parts and pieces of stainless steel welded together, the local population includes some of America's most talented welders. Many are prepared to do a bit of after-hours work in exchange for some good homebrewed beer.

Klopfer's first exposure to homebrew came from his brother Gary, a local businessman and owner of Anchorage's Snow Goose brewpub. "To test Gary's first homebrew, we included it in a blind tasting of commercial microbrewed beers," Tom said. When the homebrew held its own against the likes of Pete's Wicked Ale and Sierra Nevada Pale Ale, Tom Klopfer decided if Gary could make good-tasting beer, that he should also be making his own beer.

Although he has shared his brew with a lot of people, Klopfer is still amazed at the number of folks who come up to him and say, "I can't believe you can make beer like this."

Most recently, he served a pale ale at his daughter Jessica's wedding in New York. "I just put three soda kegs in my luggage, surrounded them with clothes, and checked them on the airplane," he says. "When we tapped them at the wedding, they were gone before I had a chance to get a second glass."

Having mastered the basics, Klopfer is now branching out. His wife, Mary, likes Belgian beers and especially lambics, so now he is trying his hand at these styles. "I've studied all the information I can find on lambics in books, on the Internet, and through the brewing magazines, but I'm still a little afraid of how they'll turn out," he says. "Still, it's fun to try something new."

When the brewing is over and it's time to sample the fruits of his labor, Klopfer enjoys his latest equipment addition: a three-tap draft tower made from an antique copper fire extinguisher. "The supply places wanted three hundred dollars for a new draft tower, but the fire extinguisher makes a perfect substitute and it only cost twenty bucks."

That must be just the kind of luck you have when you've got a burning desire to brew.

HOME-TOASTED MALT GIVES FLAVOR AND COMPLEXITY

THE SUCCESS OF MY THIRD BATCH of homebrew turned me into a die-hard beer geek. One secret of that batch was the use of freshly roasted grains.

Starting with pale ale or two-row malt, you can easily roast your own malt at home. The resulting product will enhance the flavor of your beers, giving them character and complexity other brewers will envy.

Next time you're ready to brew, fire up the oven and toast up half a pound of malt to add to your regular recipe. Use the lightest roast for pale ales and light-colored lagers; amber malt for copper to brown ales; and brown malt for porters, stouts, and bocks. The results will amaze you!

You'll need an oven, a cookie sheet (covered with aluminum foil to ease cleanup), and pale ale or two-row malt.

Place the malt on the cookie sheet to a depth of no more than half an inch. Place in the oven at 250 °F (121 °C) for about thirty minutes to dry the malt.

Next, you're ready to raise the temperature and actually toast the malt. From a practical perspective, you can hit three different levels of toastiness.

Throughout this process, you can assess the degree of toasting by comparing the cooked kernels to the uncooked ones you saved at the beginning. To compare, break open several kernels of the roasted malt and the unroasted malt, and compare the color of their starchy interiors.

First, raise the oven temperature to 300 °F (149 °C). For the lightest toast, keep the malt in for fifteen to twenty minutes at this temperature. For a medium toast, continue for a total of thirty to forty minutes. Now the interior of the kernel should be a cream or light buff color. This is approximately equal to amber malt. For additional roasting, raise the heat again, to 350 °F (177 °C), and perform a similar color check every ten to fifteen minutes. The interior of brown malt will take on a distinct tan color.

It's the Pits!   Richard had been homebrewing for about two years when he decided to buy a couple of soda kegs to ease his bottling burden. They were used but had been nicely reconditioned. Also, he got a great deal on them; the purchase didn't wreak much havoc on the household budget. From the beginning, the kegs worked like a charm.

When summer rolled around, Rich's brewing activity slowed, and eventually there came a time when he emptied a keg and had nothing new to put in it. After cleaning the keg, he filled it with his usual bleach-and-hot-water sanitizing solution and decided to let it sit overnight before emptying it.

But he got busy the next day and didn't have time to dump the sanitizing solution. He figured it wasn't a problem; he had kept the same sanitizing solution in glass fermenters for weeks at a time. He finally emptied the soda keg several weeks later. When he picked it up, he noticed a small spot on the top part of the keg—a pinpoint of black surrounded by a rough grey area. On further inspection, this turned out to be a hole in the keg! What's more, there was a line of pits inside the keg where the top of the cleaning solution had been. These pits weren't holes yet, but they certainly ruined the smooth finish of the keg, creating areas where bacteria could hide.

Rich asked around and learned that stainless steel cannot stand sustained contact with chlorine solutions. Chlorine is a great sanitizer, and even professional brewers sometimes use it with stainless steel, but it must be handled with caution. Thirty minutes of contact is usually long enough to provide the sanitizing effect. Afterward, the keg should be rinsed with plain water to take away residual bleach, unless it will be filled with beer within a few hours. Also, if a concentrated drop of bleach comes in contact with your stainless-steel items, wipe and rinse the affected area immediately!

HARD CIDER THAT'S A SNAP

ENGLISH AND AMERICAN BREWING both have a long tradition of what we Americans would call hard cider. Today you can buy alcoholic cider in many bars, but it's fun and easy to make your own!

What's needed? Mostly apple juice—but not just any juice will do. Most store-bought juices have been treated with a preservative that prevents the growth of yeast. You need natural apple juice, fresh and unfettered by chemical additives.

If you live where apples are grown, you can pick up fresh apple juice from a farm or roadside stand. This goes a long way to producing a tasty finished product.

I've also had success finding fermentable apple juice at health food stores. Look for "organic" or "natural" apple juice. It's often cloudy and has sediment on the bottom of the bottle. Read the contents and labels, looking for the words "no preservatives added."

When you find some good apple juice, pick up three to five gallons to fuel your first batch of cider. The great thing about cider is that you don't have to cook it. No slaving over a hot kettle, no hop additions to worry about, and no chilling before you can ferment. For the simplest approach, take the top off a gallon jug of apple juice, add some yeast and an airlock, and let it go.

Despite the ease of fermenting untreated juice, better cider will result with one minor addition. Most cider-makers use sugar of some sort to fortify the apple juice. The gravity of apple juice is often below that of the average wort, and finished cider benefits if its alcohol concentration is slightly higher than that of beer. As a result, some addition of fermentables is useful. Veteran cider-makers use various forms of sugar for this purpose, from plain table sugar to brown sugar to honey. Just add half a cup per gallon of apple juice before you add the yeast.

Dry Whitbread ale yeast is perfect for making cider. It ferments well and contributes to the fruity aromas of the apple juice.

Basic cider will ferment in a few weeks, but it may benefit from additional aging. Some sources suggest making the cider in the fall and leaving it in the fermenter until spring. In *The Art of Cidermaking*, champion cider-maker Paul Correnty suggests a primary fermentation of about four months, followed by a secondary of two months before bottling or serving.

At bottling time, you can make either still or sparkling cider. Still cider needs nothing added before bottling. For sparkling cider, just add half to three-fourths of a cup of corn sugar (boiled in one cup of water) for five gallons of cider, just as with beer. Then just cap, condition, and enjoy!

THE BREAKFAST (CEREAL) OF CHAMPIONS

OKAY, SO 7 A.M. is a bit early to start tasting homebrew, at least in most people's books. Still, those of you who count yourselves among the beer-obsessed know you can't keep from thinking about beer just because it's morning. Maybe that's what inspired the Chicago Beer Society (CBS) a few years ago to conduct a Breakfast Cereal Brewoff, in which every entry had to include one box (any size) of breakfast cereal.

Sound crazy? Well, maybe it was, but the resulting beers were quite tasty. We served them all at one time, and they were enjoyed by the collected homebrewers present and one very special guest, famed beer writer Michael Jackson.

The cereals ranged from Cream of Wheat and Special K to Frosted Mini-Wheats and Pop-Tart Crunch. One brewer used a tiny box from a variety pack, while another chucked in the whole super-economy-sized package. The styles of beer produced ranged from cream ales to bitters and from porters to Belgian-style abbey and brown ales. In the end, an extra special bitter brewed by CBS member Al Korzonas won both the popular vote and Jackson's favor.

Many of us thought the challenge was actually a little too easy. Had Michael Jackson not been scheduled to appear, we might have placed tighter restrictions on the cereal additions, requiring the use of a box of either Cocoa Puffs, Fruit Loops, or Cinnamon Mini Buns in every batch.

What kind of beer could you make with one of these sugar-packed breakfast treats? The only way you'll ever know is to try it! Better yet, get together with your local club and challenge a rival group to a Cereal Beer Showdown. May the best bowl of beer win!

MEAD FROM HEAVEN

BEFORE THERE WAS BEER, people probably drank mead, which is fermented honey and water. If you have a taste for honey (and most people do), it's hard to resist the charms of this most ancient of beverages.

The folklore and legends that surround mead are fantastic, featuring ancient gods that transform themselves from serpents to eagles while servicing love-starved giantesses and Viking maidens. Even more amazing are the real facts: the honey needed for one gallon of mead is the result of more than 400,000 miles of flight by bees that may have visited more than 100 million flowers in the process.

If you're lucky and know an apiarist (beekeeper), you may have already sampled the alluring essence that is mead. Now that you know something about brewing, you'll be happy to hear that mead-making is as easy as it is rewarding.

Here's a basic recipe for one gallon of mead. To craft larger-quantity recipes, multiply the specified amount of each ingredient by the total number of gallons you want to make.

MEAD (makes 1 gallon)
2.5–3 pounds clover, wildflower, or orange blossom honey
0.5–0.75 ounce acid blend (alternately, use the juice of 1 1/2 lemons)
0.07 ounce grape tannin (alternately, use 1 tablespoon of very strong tea)
Yeast nutrients as directed on package
Champagne yeast or a white wine yeast such as Sauternes or Steinberg

Use enough water to equal half the finished volume in a pot, and bring it to a boil. When the water is boiling, turn off the heat. Add the honey and all of the other ingredients except for the yeast, stirring to dissolve them in the water. This process pasteurizes the honey and mixes the ingredients. After 20 minutes, add cold water to achieve the desired volume. When the must (unfermented mead) is cool, transfer it to a fermenter and add the yeast.

Mead takes a long time to ferment and age, so be patient. Check the fermenter about once a week to see what's happening. Fermentation should be steady early on. When this has slowed and debris is collecting on the bottom of the fermenter, transfer the mead to a secondary fermenter.

When the product has aged for six months to a year in the fermenter, you can bottle it. Mead can be either still or sparkling. Still mead needs nothing added before bottling. For sparkling mead, just add 1/2 to 3/4 cup of corn sugar (boiled in 1 cup of water) for 5 gallons, just as with beer.

A year after brewing, the mead should be enjoyable. But most meads continue to mature and mellow for some time to come. For many years now, I've made one batch of mead each summer. Today, my mead cellar holds some treasures that are more than seven years old. Many have already been enjoyed by my guests and me, and some of those that remain are continuing to improve!

11

A RYE REFRESHER

RYE DOESN'T GET MUCH RESPECT in the United States. Sure, we eat a bit of it in dark bread, and once in a great while you'll find a rye whiskey to sip. Otherwise, though, rye doesn't see much action here.

In some areas of Europe, rye is a major food grain. It seems to thrive on agricultural abuse and grows where other grains wither. Because rye is the primary grain for some parts of the world, some beers rely on it as their main ingredient.

One rye-based beer is a refreshing, low-alcohol beverage called *kvass*. Made in Eastern Europe and Russia, it's considered an appropriate beverage for children as well as adults.

Three gallons of this treat can be brewed up using just a pound and a half of grain. Best of all, it's intended to be drunk fresh, so you can brew it Thursday for a picnic on Saturday!

Although no hops are used in kvass, citric acid (sometimes in the form of lemon juice) can be added to provide balance and some flavor. Other recipes add sugar, honey, or molasses, and perhaps a fist full of raisins.

I've only tasted two batches of kvass: one in Japan and one I made myself. Because Japan is close to the eastern edge of Russia, the Slavic influence is sometimes evident in European restaurants in Tokyo. The kvass I tasted was highly sweetened, like southern ice tea.

My own recipe is for the unsweetened style. It's thin, but very refreshing and thirst quenching—something you could drink a lot of. The flavor of the grain is subtle, but the acidity lends an element of balance as well as a pleasant flavor note. Brew some of this rye refresher for your next summer get-together!

KVASS (makes 3 gallons)
Target original gravity: 1.017
1 pound six-row malt
0.5 pound flaked rye
1 ounce rice hulls to aid lautering
1 package of Munton & Fisons dry ale yeast

Mix the grains with 3 quarts of water at about 150 °F (65 °C). Let stand 30 to 45 minutes. Then lauter using a large strainer positioned over a pot. Pour the mixture of grain and water into the strainer so all liquid accumulates in the pot. Sparge the grain with about a gallon of water at 160 to 170 °F (71 to 77 °C). Bring the volume in the pot to 3.25 gallons and boil 20 minutes. To flavor, add 1/4 teaspoon citric acid to the sparge water and 1/2 teaspoon to the finished product. Alternately, add lemon juice to taste in the finished product. Chill and add the yeast. This preparation will ferment completely in a day or less. After 24 to 36 hours, chill the fermenter and rack the finished kvass into a soda keg or other serving vessel. It can be served still or force carbonated in a soda keg.

◢◤ 12 ◢◤ JUST A SPOON FULL OF MALT . . .

MALTED MILK WAS POPULAR in the mid-1900s, perhaps the result of brewers having explored new markets during Prohibition. In any case, malt extract makes a tasty addition to a glass of milk. If you add a touch of sugar and a scoop of ice cream, the resulting treat will delight both children and adults.

MALTED MILK SHAKE
1 cup milk
2 tablespoons malt extract (your choice of color and form) } mix first
1 tablespoon sugar (optional)
1 ~~tablespoon~~ cup vanilla ice cream (optional) - add last

Whip these ingredients in a blender for one minute to produce a cool malty treat!

CARAMEL MALT BREAD

A SMALL MEASURE OF CARAMEL OR CRYSTAL MALT provides both flavor and texture to homemade bread. This recipe for bread will please the whole family any time of day. It also makes an attractive accompaniment to any meal where beer is served.

CARAMEL MALT BREAD (makes two small loaves or one big one)
1 cup uncrushed medium Crystal malt (40–80 °L)
1 cup hot water
3 tablespoons light or amber malt extract (dry or liquid)
1 tablespoon bread yeast
2.5–3 cups bread flour
3 tablespoons butter or margarine, melted in a small cup or bowl
1 teaspoon salt

Measure the Crystal malt into a measuring cup, and then add just enough cold water to cover the malt. Let it sit 15 minutes. Put it in a food processor and process for about a minute.

Mix a cup of hot water with 3 tablespoons of malt extract. When the extract is dissolved, add the bread yeast and mix thoroughly.

Next, mix 1.5 cups of the bread flour with the processed Crystal malt, melted butter, and water–extract–bread yeast mixture. Set it aside in a warm place to rise. Wait about 30 minutes, or until the dough has doubled in size.

Punch the dough and add a teaspoon of salt and a cup of flour. Mix these ingredients, adding more flour until the dough isn't sticky. Knead for 5 minutes, form into loaves, and place loaves in greased pans. Set aside in a warm place to rise. When the loaves have nearly doubled in size, bake for 50 minutes at 375 °F (190 °C).

Pete Slosberg—From Homebrew to National Brand

During the early 1990s, Pete's Wicked Ale became one of the first nationally known brands of craft beer. And it all started with a homebrew.

Pete Slosberg's adventures in brewing began when he moved to the San Francisco Bay area. At the time, he hated beer and instead drank wine. Interested in a new hobby, he visited the local home wine and beer shop. There he discovered he could buy the grapes used to make his favorite wine, Stag's Leap Cabernet. He quickly bought the grapes and the required wine-making equipment and whipped up his first batch.

Once the wine was safely in the fermenter, Slosberg realized he would have to wait five to ten years to enjoy the fruits of his labor. Unable to find any excitement in the years of waiting, he decided that wine-making was not his idea of a hobby. He returned to the homebrew store and asked what he could make that would be ready sooner. When the shopkeeper suggested beer, Slosberg said, "I don't like beer. I'm not interested in making beer."

But the shop owner persisted. "Have you ever had a homebrew?" he asked. "If you haven't had a homebrew, you've never had a real beer."

With this encouragement, Slosberg bought the additional equipment and ingredients needed to make homebrew and set out to make his first batch. By 1979, he was homebrewing once or twice a month and had started a homebrew club called the "Worry Worts."

"I love barbecue," says Pete, "so I arranged for most of the club meetings to take place at various barbecue places around the area."

During this time, Slosberg was marketing manager for a telephone technology company. When his product was launched, he convinced management to let him provide a commemorative beer to everyone on the team. During development, the product had been known as the "U-Project" ("U" stood for ultra-secret). "Management told me I couldn't mention any aspect of that code name in the name of the commemorative beer," says Slosberg. "To get around that, I got a picture of a sheep and called it Ewe Brew."

Most of those who drank that beer didn't know it, but Ewe Brew bottles would become valuable collectors' items. Just a few years later, a friend convinced Slosberg to join him in starting the beer company that resulted in development of the widely successful "Pete's Wicked" brand.

These days, the thing Slosberg enjoys most is educating others about beer. "Teaching people about beer flavor empowers them to buy good beer," he says. "I think people who pay five or six dollars for a six-pack want to know if it's good or not." He teaches three different programs about beer flavor to audiences that include consumers, beer retailers, and beer wholesalers.

He also continues to support homebrewing and in fact uses it as a teaching tool. Often, he rents out a brew-on-premise facility, brings in twenty or thirty people, and has them brew a beer. During the quiet times in the process, he teaches them about beer flavor.

"Homebrewing teaches people a lot about beer," he says. "They get a sense for how raw ingredients are used and the flavors they produce."

In his own company, Slosberg puts a similar emphasis on beer knowledge. "Every new employee goes through three days of training, and one of those is devoted to beer. At the end of the day, everyone has to take an exam modeled after the one used in the Beer Judge Certification Program."

Like most people who come from a homebrewing background, Slosberg enjoys lots of beer styles. He has had the opportunity to visit the beer capitals of Europe and sample their wares, from Dublin to Düsseldorf and Burton to Bamberg. "There are a lot of fantastic beers out there," he says. "The chance to sample them and to appreciate the flavors you encounter is something every homebrewer has a head start on."

MALT EXTRACT BREAD

MALT EXTRACT PROVIDES CONCENTRATED malt flavor, so just a little flavors a loaf or two of bread. This recipe yields a small loaf of smooth, malt-flavored bread you can use for sandwiches or snacks.

MALT EXTRACT BREAD (makes a small loaf)
2/3 cup hot water
3 tablespoons amber or dark malt extract (dry or liquid)
2 teaspoons bread yeast
2.5–3 cups bread flour
2 tablespoons butter or margarine, melted in a small cup or bowl
1/2 teaspoon salt

Mix the hot water with the malt extract. When the extract is dissolved, add the yeast and mix thoroughly.

Next, mix 1.5 cups of the bread flour with the melted butter or margarine and the water-extract-yeast mixture, then set aside in a warm place to rise. Wait about 30 minutes or until the dough has doubled in size.

Punch the dough and add 1/2 teaspoon of salt and a cup of flour. Mix these ingredients, adding more flour until the dough is no longer sticky. Knead for 5 minutes, form into a loaf, and place loaf in a greased pan. Set aside in a warm place to rise. When nearly doubled in size, bake 40 minutes at 400 °F (204 °C).

SPENT GRAIN COOKIES

SPENT GRAIN IS A VIABLE FOODSTUFF. Although most of the carbohydrates have been removed from the grain, a good deal of fiber and protein remain. Companies buy this spent grain from breweries, dry it, and sell it as livestock feed.

It would be hard for anyone to enjoy eating the amount of spent grain produced by the average batch of homebrew. But small portions of spent grain can be added to some foods to provide texture and visual appeal. This variation on oatmeal raisin cookies is one example where spent grains make a natural addition.

SPENT GRAIN COOKIES
6 tablespoons butter
1/4 cup table sugar
1 cup light or amber malt extract syrup
1 egg
1/2 teaspoon cinnamon
1/2 cup flour
1/4 teaspoon salt
1/4 teaspoon baking soda
1/2 cup raisins
1 cup instant oats
1/2 cup spent grains (or substitute 1/2 cup crushed fresh grain that has been covered
    with hot water and soaked 30 minutes)

Thoroughly beat together butter, sugar, malt extract, and egg. Then mix in the rest of the ingredients. Plop tablespoon-sized portions onto a cookie sheet and bake at 350 °F (177 °C) for about 15 minutes.

16 HOP COFFEE GETS YOUR MORNING GOING

HOPS IN YOUR COFFEE? You bet! Anyone who likes the flavors and aromas of hops will enjoy a pinch of them in their favorite morning brew. The trick is to add the hops to the ground coffee before brewing. That way, the flavorful hop resins and oils are extracted during the brewing process. Two or three hop cones or a couple of hop pellets will suffice when brewing four to six cups of coffee.

As for hop variety, I personally prefer the spicy flavor of Cascades. Lager lovers may find the European aroma varieties such as Saaz, Spalt, or Tettnang more inviting. Experiment and enjoy at home, or spike the office coffee pot to proclaim your fascination with beer to everyone you work with.

hops in the brew.

17 REST EASY ON A PILLOW OF HOPS

THE NATURAL AROMAS OF HOPS reportedly have a sleep-inducing effect. Hop growers and brokers say they can sometimes hardly keep their eyes open when surrounded by bales of hops during harvest or in a storage area. One hop handler I know tossed a bale in the back of his station wagon before heading off on a short trip. Within half an hour, he had to stop for some fresh air before the hops put him to sleep.

Rumor has it that European nobles made small pillows from hops to help them sleep. I know some modern brewers who have also given this a try. If you suffer from the occasional sleepless spell, you might check this out yourself. Just buy a small mesh bag and fill it with whole hops. The dried ones you get at the homebrew store will work fine, but fresh hops, if you can find them, might hold up better. Even if it doesn't cause you to fall asleep, it will help you enjoy being awake!

18 STUMP THE EXPERTS

YOU DON'T HAVE TO BE AROUND BREWERS long before you meet people who seem to really know their stuff. They've probably brewed for awhile, traveled in search of beer, and maybe done some writing about beer.

Of course, experts come in all shapes and sizes, and with all types of backgrounds. You can conduct this activity with a panel of two to four experts—whether they are Michael Jackson and Charlie Papazian or your club's best brewers.

Here's the drill. Set up a table and chairs at the front of the room for the experts. Give them a microphone if there's going to be a big crowd. Present the experts with a glass of unidentified beer. At the same time, give a sample of the beer to everyone watching. The experts' job is to work together to identify the style and, if possible, the brand of the beer. They'll taste it, discuss it among themselves, and then tell the assembled crowd what they think it is. For the exercise to be most useful, they should also say why they reached that conclusion, tying the flavors of the beer to specific characteristics of style and brand. Once the experts have guessed, bring out the bottle and tell everyone what they have just tasted.

While this contains an element of braggadocio, it's a useful way to enhance everyone's tasting skills and knowledge of beer styles. Of course, you'll have to select bottled commercial beers from both the United States and abroad, mixing in some classics and lesser-known entries. (No fair throwing in homebrew.) Remember, the people watching are playing the game too—they'll want to feel like they can make an educated guess at some of the beers. Be sure to keep the identities of the beers secret from all but one or two helpers. Store and pour the beers in another room that's off limits.

After a half dozen beers or so, everyone will have had some good fun and a few great beers. Then, let the experts off the hook and dissolve the formal setting into a pleasant stand-around bull session. I guarantee there will be plenty to talk about!

HOLD A WEIZEN BEER BRUNCH

THE TRUE BAVARIAN WEIZEN BEER is a wonderful drink that I hope you've already discovered. If not, run out to the liquor store right now, buy a bottle of imported *weizen* from the list provided in this activity, and give it a try.

If you're already among the ranks of weizen lovers, you may be looking for an excuse to enjoy some good weizens with friends. In Bavaria, weizen beer is sometimes consumed early in the day by workers. As early as 9 A.M., when even the most enthusiastic American beer lovers are still thinking about coffee, Müncheners can be seen quaffing the day's first beer.

Weizen has a healthy image in Germany because of its yeast and protein content, so perhaps this helps explain the morning ritual. Then too, the low bitterness and banana-and-clove fruitiness make weizen refreshing and easy on the palate.

On weekends, Germans around Munich may enjoy the "brunch of Bavaria," which includes weizen beer and other local specialties. The meat portion of the brunch is *weisswurst,* a white sausage made of veal and seasoned with parsley. Accompanying this is a giant soft pretzel called a *brezen* (see Idea 78: A Soft Spot for Pretzels). Add a bit of sweet mustard and perhaps a pickle or two, and you have the classic accompaniment for weizen beer.

Weizenbier, weisswurst, and soft pretzels: Mmmm. What a wonderful idea for a beer tasting! Imagine a sunny brunch in the backyard with friends or a larger gathering at your local German restaurant. Assemble the traditional foods and select one or more beers from the list below. Eat, drink, and enjoy!

A WORD ABOUT WEIZEN BEER STYLES
You'll see a number of terms used to label wheat beers, so it's useful to know what they all mean.

Weizen. Literally "wheat," this word is often used to describe the Bavarian style of wheat beer. Weizens are low in bitterness with distinct clove or banana character in the aroma and flavor. Many American brewers use this word to label their wheat beers, even though they lack the classic banana-and-clove flavor profile.

Weiss or weisse. Literally "white," this term is interchangeable with weizen used in southern Germany. In Berlin however, weiss describes a very different type of wheat beer with a tart, acidic flavor. Because of the potential for confusion, many prefer to use the term weizen when describing Bavarian-style beers.

Hefe or mit-hefe. Hefe means "yeast," and most tradi-tional-type weizens contain some yeast in suspension in the beer. This and protein from the wheat give the beer a cloudy appearance.

Kristal or Crystal. These terms describe weizens that have been filtered to be "crystal"-clear. Taste pro-file changes slightly from that of the hefeweizens.

Dunkelweizen. A darker version of the style that often has a more subdued clove-and-banana character.

Weizenbock. A weizen-style beer made to a higher gravity and alcohol content.

Commercial examples of imported weizen beers include Schneider Weisse, Paulaner, Hacker-Pschorr, Erdinger Weissbier, Ayinger Weissebier, and Franziskaner Club Weiss. American renditions of the style are Samuel Adams Wheat Beer, Samuel Adams Dunkelweizen, Frankenmuth Weisse, Gartenbrau Weizen, and Tabernash Weizen.

START A SIX-PACK CLUB

THE BEST WAY TO LEARN ABOUT BEER and improve your own brewing is to taste lots of beers. While you're at it, discuss them with others who are also interested in beer and brewing. When you first start out, you'll be learning about beer styles and developing an understanding of what you like and don't like. Also, you'll start to discover off-flavors—and find that even some high-priced beers can be in terrible shape when you get them home.

For all these reasons, it's nice if you can taste a new beer without paying for the whole six-pack. Most big liquor stores sell unusual products as single bottles. Unfortunately, this is not always the case, and even when it is, the selection of singles rarely matches the availability of six-pack products.

Enter the Six-Pack Club. To share both the cost and the experience of tasting new beers, you can form this group with two to six fellow beer brewers. Each month, the group can buy one or more six-packs and sample them at a monthly meeting. At this meeting, you could exchange notes and comments and decide what to try next. If someone in the group travels, have them pick up products that aren't available locally.

To direct your tasting, consult one of the many books on beer styles (or other activity ideas in this book), selecting a country or style to explore each month. Imagine comparing a European classic with the best of America's great brews for less than the cost of a six-pack each month!

BREW IN THE ZOO
(AND OTHER WACKY PLACES)

IF YOU ARE AN ENTHUSIASTIC HOMEBREWER, you want to share your hobby with everyone. The American Homebrewers Association® offers you a natural opportunity to do this every year on National Homebrew Day, usually held on the first Saturday of May.

Many activities in this book could be staged by a club in recognition of National Homebrew Day. This one is a natural for individuals or clubs of any size.

The idea is to brew beer in public, where you can attract attention to the hobby and to your club. Almost any public place that draws a good crowd in early May is a good candidate. But if you make it just a little wacky, you'll draw more attention—and you just might get some media attention as well. My club hasn't tackled this one yet, but Chicago has no shortage of places we could do an attention-getting brew. Famous landmarks are a natural, of course—the top of the Sears Tower, for instance, or maybe under the famous Picasso statue in Daley Center.

Or how about the museum? In addition to brewing, you could provide educational information about related topics: yeast metabolism at the science museum; the history of beer and brewing at the local history hall; water chemistry at the aquarium, oceanarium, or beach.

Another angle is to incorporate aspects of your surroundings into the brew: tips of branches from a nearby spruce tree, water from the adjacent river or lake, honey from a local hive, or even candy from the attraction's gift shop.

Finally, see if you can get some brewing help from the inhabitants of your chosen site. Use tour guides, visitors, or animals to help deliver hops to the pot or grain to the mash tun.

Planning is the key to success. Contact the prospective facility well in advance—say January or February. Set up a meeting to discuss what you want to do and what you can offer them. Be sure to let the local papers and television stations know what you're doing. Saturday is a notoriously slow news day, and they might just drop on by. Also, organize brew ingredients in advance, planning carefully so you'll have everything you need to succeed.

You may not be able to drink or serve homebrew in a public place. What you can do is schedule a party later in the day for everyone who helps. If you meet other homebrewers and prospective new club members during the day, invite them, too!

BREW UP ROOT BEER
FOR THE KIDS OR YOURSELF!

I love the way you mix your root beer with a spoon.
I love putting the sugar in and stirring it.
I love to put the molasses in the root beer with you.
I love my dad's root beer so much that I drink it every day!
I love you more than anything . . . even more than root beer.
Happy Father's Day!

—Megan Daniels, age 6

UNLESS YOU LIVE ALONE, one of the most important things you learn as a home-brewer is to share the results of your skills with your housemates. Whether you're making fruit beer for your wife or stout for your roommate, you'll find they tolerate the time and mess of brewing far better after you've served something they love.

Kids are the same way, of course, but you can't give them beer. Root beer is a nice alternative, and it's easy to make—so easy, in fact, that they can usually help.

The biggest challenge is having appropriate equipment. To carbonate and serve root beer, you need a stainless-steel soda keg. (Trying to carbonate this stuff in a bottle would be very dangerous!)

Most homebrew stores sell root beer extract along with other soda mixes. Once you have the basic flavoring, all you have to add is sugar and water. The sugar can be table sugar, corn sugar, corn syrup, honey, molasses, brown sugar, and so on. The amount you need depends on your tastes, but the basic rule of thumb is a pound or less per gallon. For me, it's a challenge to get a good level of sweetness without going overboard. At the same time, you want to impart some body so you know you're drinking something other than flavored water. I find that corn syrup and malto-dextrin help to achieve these goals.

Here's my favorite recipe.

MEGAN'S FAVORITE ROOT BEER (makes 3 gallons)
Root beer extract
1.5–3 pounds corn syrup
1 ounce malto-dextrin

Mix all ingredients in warm water. Transfer to soda keg. Chill, carbonate to about 30 psi, and serve. If you don't have a soda keg, carbonate by fermentation in 2-liter plastic soda bottles. You have to drink the root beer as soon as it's carbonated if using the soda bottles.

BARBECUE YOUR MALT FOR
THAT TANGY, SMOKED-BEER FLAVOR

BEFORE THE INDUSTRIAL REVOLUTION, when coal came into wide use, all malt had a smoky flavor. Before 1700, malt was kilned or dried above a wood fire. As it dried, it was infused with smoke. The English ales enjoyed by Mary, Queen of Scots, and Robin Hood were brown and smoke-flavored. Smoked brown malts were used not only in brown ale, they were the primary ingredient in porters and stouts when those styles emerged during the eighteenth century.

By smoking a bit of brown malt on the grill, you can produce a wonderful porter that has red highlights and an enjoyable smoked flavor. You can also add some of this malt to an Oktoberfest recipe to produce a German-style *rauchbier*. In both cases, just add three to six pounds of smoked malt to the normal recipe.

Here's the tried-and-true procedure for smoking your own brown malt using a grill. If you prefer fresh-toasted flavor without the smoke, see Idea 7 for details on oven roasting.

You'll need a charcoal grill, charcoal, wood chips (alder and apple work well, but even hickory and mesquite can be tasty), a section of metal mesh window screen or similar material (this supports the malt during heating, so it must be fire-proof and adequately strong), and pale or two-row malt (whole).

Start the charcoal fire. Put the wood chips in water to soak. After saving a few kernels for comparison, dampen the malt by soaking it a few minutes in cold water. Then spread it on the screen to a depth of one-quarter to one-half inch. (Leave some room for stirring and turning. It takes several batches to smoke a reasonable quantity of malt.) When the coals are ready, use the grill's dampers and lid to reduce the heat to a low level. Drain the wood chips and sprinkle them over the coals, and then place the malt on the grill and cover it.

Now keep an eye and an ear on your malt. Ideally it will take fifteen to twenty minutes over the smoke and heat for the malt to roast. Stir and turn it every five minutes or so, and watch for charring. Near the end, the malt may start to pop. This means it's getting dry and will probably be ready soon. If you hear popping or see charring before the ten-minute mark, the heat is too high or the malt was too dry when you started. Pull that batch off, correct the problem, and try with the next batch.

After fifteen minutes, take a few kernels of roasted malt, break them open, and compare them with the unroasted malt. The starchy endosperm of the roasted malt should begin to change color during heating. By the time it has turned light tan, the malt is done and you can remove it from the grill.

Impure as the Driven Snow One of Holland's leading homebrewers is a gentleman named Jan van Schaik. He tells the story of a fellow Netherlander who decided it would be a good idea to brew beer from snow. Accordingly, he collected a great deal of snow, filled his brewpot, and set it on the stove to melt.

BLOOPERS
#!*

This brewer believed that the snow, freshly fallen from the sky, would be pure and clean—unlike any water you could find on the ground. He (like many American consumers), believed great beer was the product of pure water. Imagine his dismay when the snow melted, revealing not crystal-clear virgin water, but a gray, murky liquid suffused with small particles of dirt.

Unfortunately, Earth's skies are not the pristine place they once were. Now falling snow and rain help to clean the sky of the dirt and pollution our industrial society has put there. But even if this weren't true, fresh rain or melted snow would not be ideal for brewing, because they lack the mineral content needed during mashing and fermentation.

THINKING SMALL: TEST BATCH BREWING

IN A LARGE PART, it's experimentation that makes brewing fun. After you've made half a dozen recipes or so, you'll start to wonder, "What would happen if I did this?" Some of the most wonderful beers ever made were created because of that exact thought process.

Because the results are often wonderful, some folks like to conduct their experiments at the full five-gallon scale. When the brews turn out well, they have plenty to drink and share. But when experimental results are less than ideal, it makes for a lot of leftover beer.

To avoid large surpluses of experimental beer, I try new ideas in small batches. If I'm really in unknown territory (trying to develop a carrot beer like Idea 99, for instance), I make batches as small as a gallon.

You can make a one-gallon all-grain beer using the masher described in Idea 6: Longing to Lauter. It will hold up to five pounds of grain, giving you enough capacity to make one gallon of normal to very strong all-grain beer, or perhaps two gallons of a lower-gravity brew.

For fermenters, use one-gallon glass juice jugs. Apple juice is sometimes sold in these containers, although plastic is rapidly taking over. I have about ten glass jugs, and there are always a couple sitting around with something interesting in them.

Now let's say you want to make an unusual style like rauch (smoked) beer and have just smoked five pounds of malt on the grill. You're ready to brew with it, but don't know how much malt to use. One solution is to make a one-gallon test batch, using the same grain proportions you plan for the full-scale batch. If you plan to use a special yeast for the beer, the one-gallon batch can also serve as a yeast starter!

Using this approach, you should be able to make and ferment the test batch and test its flavor. To achieve the flavor you want, adjust the amount of smoked malt and brew a full-scale batch that will be closer to your goals.

YEAST: IT TAKES ALL TYPES

OUR FRIEND *Saccharomyces cerevisiae* gets little respect as a brewing ingredient from the world at large. The average Joe figures all brewers use identical yeast. And who can blame him? If you believe the advertising, water is more important than yeast to beer flavor.

Even brewers don't give yeast its due. Every brewer I know claims to make beer. But in truth, brewers make unfermented wort. That wort isn't beer until it contains alcohol. What makes that alcohol? The yeast, of course.

Anyone who has brewed a few batches knows homebrew stores sell lots of different yeasts. From the macro view, all yeasts do the same thing—eat sugar and produce alcohol and carbon dioxide. So why are there so many different types?

The answer, ultimately, is flavor. Each strain of brewers' yeast processes wort nutrients slightly differently at a chemical level. The wide range of flavor compounds produced by yeast appears in different ratios depending on the yeast strain. As a result, selection of a yeast strain for a recipe can be the most important decision a brewer makes.

Maybe you don't believe me—I know I was skeptical the first time I heard all this. But you can prove it to yourself fairly easily, and here's how.

Make a batch of beer. When it's time to ferment, split the batch into three to five equal-sized portions in separate fermenters (one-gallon apple juice jugs make excellent small fermenters). Pitch each fermenter with a different strain of yeast. When all the batches are done and ready to drink, compare the flavors produced by each strain. Some suggestions for different strains (ale only) are given below.

FOR A PALE ALE WORT:

- American or Chico ale yeast (Wyeast 1056)
- Whitbread ale yeast (Wyeast 1098)
- ESB or London yeast (Wyeast 1968)
- Irish ale yeast (Wyeast 1084)
- European ale yeast (Wyeast 1338)

FOR A WHEAT BEER WORT:

- American or Chico ale yeast (Wyeast 1056)
- Weihenstephan *weizen* yeast (Wyeast 3068)
- Belgian *witbier* yeast (Wyeast 3944)
- *Kölsch* yeast (Wyeast 2565)

BEAT THAT! BREWOFFS
LEVEL THE PLAYING FIELD

A FEW YEARS BACK, fellow Chicago Beer Society (CBS) member Tim Norris had a great idea. He wanted to give a bunch of brewers an identical set of ingredients and tell them to make a beer. The results would be judged, and a winner declared, based on who made the best beer using those ingredients.

CBS first implemented Tim's idea in 1993. It was later adopted as part of the American Homebrewers Association's National Homebrewers Conference.

The fixed set of ingredients generally included some base malt, but not enough to produce a regular-strength beer. To reach a gravity of 1.040 or better, the brewer had to use some of the ingredient kit's extract and specialty grains. In addition, we usually allowed brewers to add a limited amount of one other ingredient— for instance, up to a pound of honey. The hops were limited to those in the kit, and we often employed little-known varieties to keep the brewers on their toes.

During the three years we did this, between fifteen and thirty beers were entered each time. All entries were tasted at a two-hour walk-around session, where people tasted and evaluated each beer at their own pace. At the end, everyone voted for their favorite, and we presented awards.

You might think all the beers would taste nearly the same, but they didn't. Because brewers could choose their own yeast strain, the character of the beers varied widely. One year, identical ingredients produced the following styles: brown ale, honey lager, Flanders golden, Belgian strong, *rauch*, American pale ale, Märzen, Scottish export, trippel, extra special bitter, pepper brown ale, and strong ale.

This type of event can be fun for half a dozen brewers in one small club or for scores of clubs in a region. Alternately, you might agree on a materials list with friends nationwide and ship samples of the finished beers for comparison.

FLAVOR ENCOUNTER: EAU DE SKUNK

BREWERS DON'T TALK ABOUT IT MUCH, but there's a common beer flavor fault that you may remember from a walk in the woods.

Skunkiness in beer is a trait that has been around ever since brewers started bottling. It happens when a certain wavelength of light interacts with hop elements in your beer. This interaction causes a chemical reaction that produces a skunklike flavor compound.

The specific wavelength in question is blocked by brown glass, but not by clear or green glass. This is the main reason you commonly see beer in brown bottles all over the world.

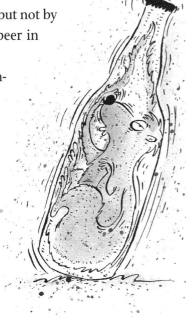

In the United States, green bottles have become a popular symbol of a brand's imported—and therefore usually premium-priced—status. Yet many beers sold here in green bottles are sold in their homelands in the more practical brown bottles.

It's easy to investigate this phenomenon. Buy an imported beer in green bottles. But instead of purchasing the six-pack displayed on the shelf or in the cooler, get one from an unopened case. This will ensure the beer hasn't already become skunked by being exposed to either sunlight or fluorescent light.

At home, put four of the bottles in a cool, dark place. Your refrigerator will do just fine. Set the other two bottles in direct sunlight. After fifteen to twenty minutes, take one bottle out of the sun, label it, and put it in the refrigerator with the others. After the sixth bottle has spent sixty minutes or so in the sun, label it and put it in the refrigerator. After all six bottles are chilled, take out the two skunked samples and one of the unskunked bottles. Pour the beers into three identical glasses.

By comparing the unskunked sample with the sixty-minute sample, you should get a clear sense of what green bottles and sunlight can do to beer. Then, when you understand the character of the skunky flavor, see if you can detect it at the lower concentration in the fifteen-minute bottle.

Warning: this exercise may ruin your appreciation of green-bottled imported beers. Once you learn to detect the skunkiness, you'll find it's often present in store-bought beers.

Randy Mosher—Creative Force

Randy Mosher makes his living as a graphic designer, creating innovative images for everything from consumer packaged goods to company logos. But this creative urge carries over into his brewing, too.

"I've made beer with a lot of crazy stuff," says Mosher. "First, there was quinoa and spelt, grains of paradise and Curaçao orange peel. It got *really* nuts after that."

One of Mosher's most famous beers was made with chanterelle mushrooms. "The chanterelles give it an incredible apricot character," he says. More recent efforts included smoked wheat malt and juniper berries as he tried to recreate some obscure European farm beers.

PROFILE

How does he find the stuff he puts in beer, you might ask? "Roam around a lot," says Mosher. "I'll go into any store that has something to do with food just to see what they have that might be used in making beer. Mexican markets are great. They have some concentrated fruit syrup that's perfect for beer. They also have some really unusual raw sugars that could provide a lot of flavor as well as fermentables. Health-food stores are great, too. If you can find a shop that specializes in spices, you'll find some really cool stuff to experiment with."

Mosher's creativity isn't limited to the brewing itself. It extends to the before and after as well. "Some people say brewing is my second hobby," admits Mosher. "My real passion is making brewing equipment."

Mosher's stated goal is to create a totally automated homebrewing system. "I want to sit at my computer upstairs, type on the keyboard, and have the system crank out a beer down here."

Lack of an engineering degree doesn't seem to hamper his mastery of the basic brewery building trades. The latest version of his wort grant is fitted with one-inch tri-clover fittings on either side and plumbed to the lauter tun, *vorlauf* return, and the feed to the boil kettle. Best of all, he has rigged a level detecting sensor to turn on a small magnetically coupled centrifugal pump when the liquid nears the top. All the parts and pieces cost him just fifty bucks—he welded and wired the whole system himself.

To sustain the equipment-building process, he enrolls in a local welding course each year to have access to equipment he needs to cut and meld stainless steel. Recently he built a fifteen-gallon cylindro-conical fermenter for his home system.

When he has a quiet moment, he sits down at his computer and cranks out arresting names and eye-catching labels for his offbeat beers. Examples include Dick's Elixir, Beelzebub Dark Cherry Ale, and Pudgy McBuck's Celebrated Cocoa Porter.

"There are just an incredible number of ways to have fun with homebrewing," says Mosher. "I've been at it for thirteen years, and I'm still finding new things to do."

MALT WAFFLES

BY NOW YOU'VE PROBABLY GUESSED that I believe a spoonful of malt can improve just about anything you eat. When the time comes for weekend waffles, you can improve their flavor in two ways with malt.

For starters, add malt extract syrup to your waffle mix. A tablespoon in three cups of batter will do. Cooking time remains about the same, and the resulting waffles are just a tad darker and slightly crisper than normal.

To make these waffles into a really malty treat, mix up some malt syrup. Add a tablespoon of malt extract to a cup of maple syrup, mix thoroughly, slather on top of the waffles, and enjoy.

If you insist on a beer to go with this wonderful concoction, you might try a cream stout. Mmm!

HALF-WIT CHICKEN

THE BELGIAN SPECIALTY beer known as *wit* (or "white") beer is usually made with spices in addition to the usual beer ingredients. This recipe uses two of the three spices often found in wit beer, namely Curaçao orange peel and grains of paradise. But in a serious case of spice dyslexia, I used cardamom instead of coriander when testing this idea. The result was so tasty I decided to go with it!

The basic idea is to make a marinade using wheat malt extract and spices. Once the meat has soaked for awhile, it can be grilled or baked. Here's the recipe for the marinade:

HALF-WIT CHICKEN
1/2 cup wheat malt extract
1/2 cup water
1/4 teaspoon cardamom seed
1/2 teaspoon Curaçao orange peel
6 grains of paradise

Crush or coarse-grind the spices to help release their flavors, then mix all the ingredients together. Marinate 1 pound of chicken (or other meats, if you want to experiment) for about an hour. While the meat is in the marinade, pierce each piece with a fork 8 to 10 times.

On a moderately heated grill, cook boneless chicken breasts 5 to 7 minutes on each side. Brush the uncooked side with marinade before you turn. In a 350-°F (177-°C) oven, bake the chicken in the marinade for 20 to 30 minutes. The finished chicken is tasty either hot or cold.

CHECK YOUR SANITY

SOME HOMEBREWERS WORRY too much. Concerned that their beer will turn out bad, they spend all their time thinking of things to worry about. For these hypochondriacs of beer, the biggest bugaboo is infection—as in "Yech, this beer is infected!"

Many unpleasant flavors in beer can be traced to runaway growth of some bacteria or foreign yeast. To avoid such problems, extreme—if misguided—measures have been employed.

One brewer I know worked at a hospital. He used sterile surgical drapes to cover his brewing area and wore sterile latex gloves while he brewed. Everything that touched the beer got dipped in alcohol first.

Everybody has a bad batch once in awhile. But if you follow reasonable sanitation practices and pitch enough yeast, you should have little to worry about.

What are reasonable sanitation practices, you ask? The actual activities are too tedious to detail here, but there's a way to learn if you're doing okay.

Some call this a sanitation test, but I call it a *sanity* test. Because once you've done this, you'll know where you stand. If you pass this test, you don't have to lie awake nights worrying about your next batch. Here's the drill.

Next time you brew, save a sample of your unpitched wort in a sterile, covered container. If it lasts a week without signs of spontaneous fermentation or bacterial growth, you'll know you've done a good job with sanitation.

The container can be any glass jar that holds eight to twenty ounces. Clean it thoroughly and remove its labels. About the time you start boiling your wort, sanitize the jar by filling it with your hottest tap water and a tablespoon of bleach. Let this sit thirty minutes or so, dropping a square piece of aluminum foil into the solution for the last five minutes. During this time, boil enough water to fill your jar twice. When the water is boiling (wear rubber gloves to protect your hands), pour out the bleach solution and overfill the jar with boiling water. Be sure the jar is in your sink or another protected area with a drain while you fill it. This gives the extra water a place to run off and some protection if the jar breaks. Put the foil square on top of the jar and crimp it down lightly. Set the bottle aside to cool.

When you're ready to transfer your wort to the fermenter, empty the hot water from the sterile jar and replace the foil cover. If the jar is too hot to hold with your bare hand, let it cool a few more minutes before you add the wort.

Ideally, add wort to the jar in the same way (pouring, racking, etc.) you add it to your fermenter. Also, if possible, make the addition to the sterile jar in the middle of the wort transfer, rather than at the beginning or the end. Cover the full jar with the foil and crimp the foil down tightly all around.

Now set the jar near your fermenter and check it daily. If you see activity or growth in the jar after just a day, you need to work some more on your sanitation procedures. If you go three or four days with no signs of activity, you're okay. If nothing happens in the sterile jar for a week or more, you're in good shape.

YOU WILL SEE CLEARLY NOW . . .

. . . ONCE THE HAZE IS GONE FROM YOUR BEER.

A lot of great-tasting homebrews aren't much to look at. Some don't have much foam on top, and a good number range from hazy to downright cloudy. If haze hazing from your friends or colleagues is spoiling your enjoyment of home-brewing, read on. You'll find ways to tackle the challenge.

Haze is an age-old problem for brewers. When we drank dark grog from stone or wooden mugs, it really didn't matter. But in the mid-1800s, when glass drinking containers and pale beers came into vogue, the issue of clarity became more important.

Beer haze comes from two natural sources: yeast and malt protein. Both play critical roles in the production of good beer, but both need to be controlled or removed at the end of the process if the product is to be clear.

Big brewers usually just filter their beer. Homebrewers with a little patience can often achieve the desired effect just by letting the beer settle for awhile. Some yeast settles more slowly than others, but most eventually drifts to the bottom of the fermenter or bottle. After primary fermentation, if you transfer your beer to a glass fermenter for secondary fermentation and settling, you can often see the beer clear from the top down. When the whole fermenter is clear, you're ready to bottle.

But even after a couple weeks of patient waiting, some beers just won't clear. Usually they have some sort of excess protein problem. If you're a staunch follower of the German purity law, *Reinheitsgebot,* you're going to be drinking some hazy beer. If you're less finicky and like clear beer, add a spoonful of finings to your beer.

Homebrew stores sell a variety of finings intended for yeast and protein. Silica gel seems to be best for protein removal. One form of it is sold under the brand name Polyclar. Add two teaspoons of this to your beer after the yeast has settled out, and it will clarify within a few hours. Afterward, rack, carbonate, and enjoy!

32

IN THE TEMPERATE ZONE

CONTROLLING FERMENTATION temperature is one way to ensure great beer. Sure, most ales are happy between 62 and 72 °F (17 and 22 °C), and lagers need a chilly 50-°F (10-°C) environment. Other styles—like *weizen, kölsch, alt,* cream ale, and even California common—also demand special temperatures.

You can conquer your refrigerator by putting a temperature controller on it. These are available from most homebrew shops for around fifty dollars. Best of all, they plug right into the wall, and the fridge plugs into them—so temperature control becomes possible even when the fridge is not your own.

If you'd rather find another way to keep your cool, try these two ideas:

CHEST COOLER FERMENTER JACKET
I found a fifty-four-quart plastic ice chest that, standing on end, was wide and deep enough to hold a five-gallon fermenter. It wasn't quite tall enough for the fermenter, much less the airlock. No problem—just cut a hole in the cooler. A four-inch-square hole in the end leaves enough room to tilt the fermenter in. During fermentation, I add some of those reusable blue ice blocks around the fermenter to keep things cool. It works fine for summertime ale fermentations.

AIR CONDITION YOUR FERMENTER
You can use a cardboard box and a length of dryer duct to create a cool zone fed by a central or window air-conditioning unit. Set up the duct so cool air is forced into it from the air conditioner or a regular room duct. Attach the other end to a box that fits over your fermenter. Create a place for the cool air to exit the box, and away you go. I know someone who claimed this system kept his fermenting beer at 60 °F (15 °C) even when the room temperature was 80 °F (27 °C).

33
DIAL-A-HOMEBREW PROJECT

IF YOU'RE STUMPED about what to brew, here are some ideas. Just look down the list for the current month and then across to the beer style you should brew. Consult your favorite treasury of beer recipes for guidance, and then get to brewing! When brewed in the month indicated, each beer should be ready to drink during its proper season. Enjoy!

	FOR BASIC BREWING		FOR ADVANCED BREWING	
MONTH	**STYLES**	**READY TO DRINK**	**STYLES**	**READY TO DRINK**
January	English pale ale	February–March	Barley wine	One year later
February	Brown porter	March–April	Maibock	May
March	Oktoberfest	September–October	Cream ale	April–June
April	Ordinary bitter	May	Smoked beer	June–July
May	Kölsch	June	Strong Scotch ale	Late fall
June	American wheat	July	Belgian ale	Fall–winter
July	Mead	One year later	Robust porter	Fall
August	Fruit beer	September on	Dunkelweiss	Fall
September	American pale ale	October–December	Doppelbock	March
October	Christmas ale	November–December	Lambic	One year later
November	Russian stout	3–12 months later	California common beer	January–February
December	Brown ale	June–February	Schwartzbier	March–June

Chuck Skypeck—Home Innovation Drives Commercial Success

In the dozen years since he started homebrewing, Chuck Skypeck has been involved in nearly every aspect of the craft-beer business. Having sold homebrew supplies and fostered homebrew events in the mid-South, he now directs brewing at the Boscos brewpubs in Nashville and Germantown, Tennessee. Yet he still homebrews.

"I have not forgotten my roots," he says, "or the roots of the craft-brewing movement in the United States."

PROFILE

Most early American craftbrewers learned their trade at home. Their experiments with ingredients, yeasts, and flavors at a low-risk homebrew scale allowed more innovative and successful beers when they began to brew commercially.

"If I'm not homebrewing, I miss it," Skypeck says. "Even though I have a lot of leeway in my commercial brewing, there is still an element of creativity that just isn't possible." At present, most of his homebrewing equipment resides at the brewpub, where he uses it to whip up pilot brews and special projects.

One recent homebrew project was a brew with the local Memphis homebrew club. With the help of the Boscos mash tun, they brewed forty-five gallons of barley wine and then squirreled it away in a whiskey barrel for aging. Because Tennessee limits commercial beers brewed in the state to no more than 5 percent alcohol, Skypeck will never be able to brew a similar beer for the pub.

Despite such limitations, he has managed to metamorphose one of his most successful and flamboyant homebrews into a popular commercial beer. Skypeck, along with buddy Phil Rahn, pioneered the brewing of stone beers as a homebrewer. (See Idea 36: Toss Some Rocks in Your Beer.) Today, he uses hot rocks to make the same type of beer at both of his Tennessee brewpubs.

"It is a unique beer that has broad appeal," Skypeck says. He describes the beer as being a "blonde *alt*" with a distinct caramel character that comes from the hot rocks. The original gravity is 1.048, and its International Bitterness Unit reading is 15. "Customers love it because they feel they are getting something special. I love it because it is a neat home-brewing project that turned into something important for our brewpub."

As Skypeck's commercial brewing explores new areas such as cask ales, the homebrew background comes in handy. "I'm splitting off a barrel of wort here and there to experiment with new yeasts or dry hopping," he says. "That allows me to keep learning and keep improving the beers we offer our customers."

"We are constantly looking for something new," he says. "Both the experience and the attitude of homebrewing help me to meet that challenge on an ongoing basis."

JUDGES' CORNER

NEXT TIME YOUR HOMEBREW group gets together, set up a judges' corner where two or three judges can have some peace and quiet. Equip them with the usual judging paraphernalia: score sheets, pencils, water pitchers, tasting cups, and maybe even some bread to cleanse their palates between beers.

Anyone can bring a beer to the judges for evaluation and tell them what style they want it judged as. They can then watch and listen as the judges evaluate the beer. Afterward, the judges may want to ask the brewer questions so they can better understand the flavors of the beer.

This is a good exercise for both brewers and judges. The brewers get an objective, considered assessment of their beer from knowledgeable people. This will help them improve their brewing and may help them decide whether to enter a beer into a competition. Meanwhile, the judges get in some extra practice. If they encounter something they don't understand or don't expect, their dialogue with the brewer can help to expand their own knowledge.

CHALLENGE YOUR TASTE BUDS

I RAN INTO THIS TEST at the National Saké Center in Tokyo. It was set up as a way to evaluate *saké* judges, but our host somehow convinced the Center to let us try and conduct the test. Basically, you taste five similar products labeled 1 through 5 at one table. You can taste as much as you want for as long as you want, but once you leave the first table you can't go back. At the second table, the same five products are presented in a different order and labeled A through E. The challenge is to match up the two sets on your scorecard.

I like to run this test with American mass-market lagers like Budweiser, Miller, and Coors. Because of the subtle flavors in these beers, it can be a real challenge to get them straight. An easier test might use all-malt Pilseners or perhaps pale ales or even stouts. To set it up, you'll need five beers in the same style, ten identical containers from which to serve the beer (anything from paper cups to pitchers), two tables or serving areas, and 3-by-5 cards for the tasters.

Label five serving containers with the numbers 1 through 5; label five more with the letters A through E. Select a number and letter for each beer and then fill the proper serving containers. Be sure to record the number and letter used for each beer.

Set the containers in the two serving areas, and let the participants go at it. Ask them to write the numbers 1 through 5 down the left margin of their 3-by-5 card while they're at the first table. At the second table, they should write a letter next to a number based on which beers they think are the same.

This is a great way to exercise your taste buds while having a little beery fun!

TOSS SOME ROCKS IN YOUR BEER

AND I'M NOT KIDDING, either. Rocks—the hard kind made of stone—have a place in brewing. Long ago, brewing vessels were made of wood, so you couldn't burn a fire under them to heat water or wort. Instead, you heated rocks in a fire and then transferred them (carefully!) into the pot to provide the heat.

In Germany today, there's a brewery that still uses hot rocks in its brewing process. The rocks are heated to red hot and then dropped into the boil kettle. As they heat the wort, a coating of caramelized sugar forms on them. After the boil is complete, the rocks are removed and put in the secondary fermenter, where they provide a source of residual sugar for the yeast to ferment as the beer ages. The rocks also release caramelized flavors, as well as some smokiness from the wood fire that heated them.

Homebrewers have used hot stones in a similar way to reproduce this brewing technique in their backyards. (Chuck Skypeck of Boscos in Nashville, Tennessee, has even translated this into a brewpub product.) The key is to acquire rocks that will be physically and chemically stable. Avoid anything with limestone (calcium carbonate); it will dissolve in the acidic wort. Also, you'll probably have to test your rocks to see which ones hold up to heat without chipping and breaking. You should be able to heat the rocks on a rack placed over a bed of hot coals. To enhance the smoky character of the brew, sprinkle the hot coals with wet oak chips.

PASS THE MALT: A MALT TASTING

MALT IS AN ESSENTIAL INGREDIENT of beer, yet too often we overlook its importance. Until this century, most brewers were also maltsters. They bought raw barley and did everything necessary to turn it into beer.

"Base malt" is the term applied to the primary malt used in a recipe. This is usually Pilsener or pale ale malt; American examples may be called simply two-row or six-row malt. Because all of these malts are used in the same way as the base for a beer recipe, people tend to think that they all taste the same. But if they did, there would be less variation in beers around the world. By tasting several different kinds of malt, you can appreciate the influence a simple change in base malt might have on your beer's flavor.

Here's what you'll need:

1 pound British pale ale malt
1 pound German Pilsener malt
1 pound American six-row malt
1 pound American two-row malt (optional)
A big glass of water

Start out by looking carefully at the malts. Notice that the six-row malts are smaller and occasionally a bit twisted. They're also typically somewhat darker than two-row American malt. English pale ale malts are usually dried at a higher temperature than other base malts, so they are most often noticeably darker. European Pilsener malts are often quite pale, and of the group they may be the lightest in color.

If you have a real eye for detail, you may notice differences in structure and shape among the three types of two-row malt: the depth of the crease, the shape of the ends, and so on. These differences are indicative of the different varieties of barley used in making these malts.

Start your tasting of each malt by biting or breaking one or two kernels in half. With the six-row malt, you'll notice that the white chalky area known as the endosperm has a smaller cross section than the other malts have. Also, look for differences in color among the starchy areas.

The Pilsener malt may have a small, shiny, glassy area that's hard when you bite it. This is the compact starch and protein matrix native to the raw barley. In most malts, this area is completely broken down ("modified" is the brewing term) during malting. Because Pilsener malts aren't always allowed to germinate for as long, these "under-modified" areas are sometimes found near the pointed end of the kernel.

Now it's time to really taste the malt. For each variety, pop five to ten kernels into your mouth and chew. Notice the level of sweetness. Look for "toasted" flavors like bready, biscuity, or crusty. Also, think about how much husky or grainy character you perceive.

In addition to flavor, notice how the malt feels: the amount of husk, how soft the kernels are, and whether they contain any hard, glassy portions.

If you're so inclined, take notes as you go to help you remember differences. Take a swig of water between samples to help separate the flavors and wash down the husks. (Don't let the husks annoy you; just think of them as healthful fiber.)

By the time you've finished tasting the malts you selected, you'll probably be amazed by the differences. The next step might be to try making several "single-malt" beers that are identical except for the malt used. If you do, be sure to share the results with other brewers so you can expand their knowledge as well as your own.

A JOLLY ALE FOR OLD SAINT NICK

CHRISTMAS HAS BEEN A TIME OF CELEBRATION in the Christian world for many centuries. In the weeks before Christmas, many special treats are unveiled—food, clothing, ceremony, and of course gifts. It's only natural for brewers to produce a special treat for this time of year—a beer that will warm both heart and body.

In Europe, Christmas beers have generally been stronger versions of the brewery's regular products. Thus we see *doppelbock* and *weizenbock* at Christmastime in Germany, as well as Christmas ales and winter warmers in the British Isles. Although holiday beers aren't the type you quaff throughout an entire evening, they should present a pleasant balance of flavors that leave you wanting more. Strong beers and those using spices can take months, even years, to reach peak drinking condition. If you brew a potent holiday batch in January or February, it has time to mature before consumption. If fall is in the air and you've yet to start your holiday treat, a more moderate approach would be wise.

Here's a three-gallon recipe for holiday spiced ale that I've enjoyed in years past. The basic recipe should have an original gravity of about 1.070, and it can be made in early fall for consumption the same year. If you're planning ahead by six months or more, add two more pounds of dry extract (or five more pounds of grain) to boost the gravity up to the 1.095–1.100 range.

HOLIDAY SPICED ALE (makes 3 gallons)
Expected original gravity: 1.070–1.075
1.5 pounds pale ale malt
2 pounds Crystal malt (medium color: 40–80 °L)
4 pounds light malt extract syrup

1 ounces Kent Goldings or Willamette hops (use 2 ounces if you add the previously mentioned extra malt)

2 ounces Cascade hops (to be added in two additions)

1/2 teaspoon allspice

1/4 teaspoon ground clove

1 teaspoon cinnamon

2 seeds cardamom

2 tablespoons grated lemon zest (grate the peel from the outside of a whole lemon)

American ale yeast

Mini-mash the grains, or soak them in water at 145 to 155 °F (63 to 68 °C) for an hour. Use a grain bag or remove them with a strainer. Add the extract and Goldings or Willamette hops, and bring to a boil. If necessary, add water to adjust your boil volume to 3.5 gallons or the capacity of your brewing pot. After boiling 55 minutes, add a tablespoon of lemon zest (reserving the second) plus all the other spices and an ounce of Cascade hops. Boil 5 more minutes and turn off the heat. Now add the final tablespoon of lemon zest and the final ounce of Cascade hops. Steep for 5 minutes and then begin your usual chilling procedure.

MALT EXTRACT EVALUATION

MAKING GREAT BEER IS EASY when you understand your ingredients. Most homebrewers use malt extract in their brews, but they know very little about it. You can vastly improve your brewing results just by running a simple test on the extracts you use.

In an extract test, you make a small batch of beer so you can evaluate the flavor and fermentability you're likely to achieve with an extract before you brew the full batch. It involves a bit of work, but you only need to do it once for each extract you use.

Make a one-quart batch of beer using just five to six ounces of liquid extract or four to five ounces of dry extract. (This doesn't need to be boiled for long—ten or fifteen minutes will do.) When cool, take an original gravity reading and pitch with an ample quantity of yeast—preferably the yeast you use most often.

To ensure full fermentation of the sample wort and to speed the process, you should pitch an excess of yeast. In the past, I've used one seven-gram packet of dry ale yeast in a gallon of wort. The resulting fermentation starts within two hours or less and is usually done within twenty-four hours. If you want to use liquid yeast for this test, simply consider this to be a yeast starter and pitch one or two swollen pouches of liquid yeast into your quart of wort. After the experiment is finished, save the yeast in the refrigerator (for up to three weeks) to use in your next full-scale batch.

When fermentation is complete, chill the beer in your refrigerator to help drop the yeast out of suspension. Measure the final gravity and calculate the apparent attenuation. A beer with an original gravity (OG) of 1.048 and a final gravity (FG) of 1.015 would have an apparent attenuation of 68.75 percent. Apparent attenuation is calculated by this formula: (OG–FG/[OG–1]) and expressed as a percentage.

Taste the finished beer to assess the flavor of the extract. In good extracts you should recognize flavors like those you get when you chew raw pale ale malt.

Also, note the color of the finished product. The colors used to describe malt extracts are somewhat euphemistic. You'll predict the finished color of your beers better if you know how much color comes from the extract alone.

This technique lets you begin to understand the differences between extracts. After a few tests, you should be able to identify one or two extracts that give good flavor and predictable results. Be sure to keep a record of the results for each brand you test.

A Shattering Experience Gina had brewed several beers, but she was still learning about the science of brewing. She knew specific gravity readings changed with the temperature of the beer or wort, because the density of a liquid changes as its temperature changes. The chart that came with the hydrometer showed correction factors for temperatures between 32 and 120 °F (0 and 49 °C), but she had recently found a book that gave corrections all the way up to the boiling point. She was amazed to see that boiling wort would give a reading 0.040 lower than its actual gravity. She couldn't wait to try it out.

A week later, she was nearing the end of her first all-grain batch, when she remembered the hydrometer correction factors. Before cutting off the heat under the boiling wort, she decided to check its specific gravity. She gently set the hydrometer into the pot, only to hear a loud crack as it split in two and sank into the turbulent wort. Too late she realized she had exceeded the operating temperature range of her hydrometer. In the future, she would put a sample of the boiling wort in the freezer for a few minutes, allowing it to reach a more moderate temperature before she took a reading.

MIX UP YOUR OWN BEER COCKTAILS

BEER COCKTAILS AREN'T A HOT ITEM these days, but they're a standard of the genre going back hundreds of years.

Probably the best known is the black and tan. Originally, this was probably equal parts bitter and either stout or porter. Today pale ale or even Pilsener might be substituted for the bitter. This combination was once so popular that commercial products today are still called "Black and Tan."

The blending of beers has many other precedents. Porter was originally a mixture of three different types of beer. Belgian *lambics* are still commonly produced by blending different batches and vintages. And cream ale, of course, is reputed to have started as a blend of lager and ale.

Publican Judy Ashworth of the Lyons Brewery in Dublin, California, raised the art of beer blending to new heights during the 1980s. Here are a few of the concoctions she created (Loysen 1990, 1–6). The names are almost as much fun as the mixtures themselves.

Foggy Night in the Sierrås: Half Anchor Old Foghorn and half Sierra Nevada Pale Ale

Trembling Fox: Half San Andreas Kit Fox Amber and half San Andreas Earthquake Porter

Anchor's Aweigh: A twenty-three-ounce glass with a lemon wedge at the bottom, filled three-quarters full with Anchor wheat beer and topped with Anchor's Old Foghorn

Purist brewers object to beer blending out of respect for the brewer's art. Judy's one rule was that each beer in the blend should be clearly detectable and not submerged or lost in the blend.

Of course, we homebrewers, occasionally want to dilute—if not lose altogether—the flavors of some beers. Blending opens up a whole new world. Blending could be an effective way to drink a beer that you really don't enjoy. Imagine that the pale ale you made is way too bitter for your taste. No problem—just blend it with a bit of *bock* beer for a smooth, well-balanced product you can enjoy.

The broader the range of beers you brew, the more blending you can do. I love both smoked beers and *weizens,* and I've had some success brewing both types. When I have one of each available, I love to mix them half and half. The smokiness and the weizen's cloviness fit together nicely for a unique and flavorful beer. (You might call it "smoke gets in your *weisse.*")

Experiment with your own beer cocktails at home or with a group. The more people in attendance, the more beers you can work with and the more cocktails you can create. One fun homebrew club event would be for everyone to bring a beer for blending: a pale ale here, a porter there; one barley wine, one bock; Jim brings a weizen and Jill brings a Pils. Over the course of an evening, I bet everyone will create at least one memorable concoction. The resulting recipes would be a great addition to the club newsletter.

COCK ALE IF YOU DARE

HISTORICAL SOURCES SITE many recipes for cock ale, a beverage whose ingredients include an old rooster. The thought of it is a bit, ahem, foul, but such drinks were once believed to have strengthening and restorative characteristics.

Generally speaking, meat in any form doesn't make a very good addition to beer. Meat contains lots of proteins and fats that don't ferment and won't dissolve in the beer. Exactly what the cock added to these early brews, I can't quite fathom.

One thing the old recipes do show is the liberal use of spices. Several call for both raisins and mace. Typically, about ten gallons of ale would be produced using a single cock, three to four pounds of raisins, and three or four blades of mace. Still other recipes suggest the addition of nutmeg, anise, rosemary, caraway seeds, lemon peel, and hart's horn (Renfrow 1994, 15–16).

What is a modern homebrewer to do with this? Spice ale, perhaps—a basic pale ale with two pounds of raisins and a quarter teaspoon of mace thrown in a few minutes before the end of the boil. Or perhaps you'd like to approach it in reverse, by putting a little beer in your chicken soup. Hmm. How about a measure of Sierra Nevada pale ale or Guinness stout added to a can of Campbell's chicken noodle?

Maybe you should consider this option the next time you're crowing for a snack. Also, see Idea 74: Wort-Crusted Chicken.

LOB SOME FRUIT INTO YOUR BEER

IT USED TO BE YOU COULDN'T GET A BEER made with fruit unless you made it yourself. Some argue that you still can't get a good fruit beer unless it's homemade, and I tend to agree. Traditionally, alcoholic beverages made from fruit were called wine. But when fruit is added to beer, the resulting beverage is a bit of an orphan— something neither brewers nor vintners have fully mastered.

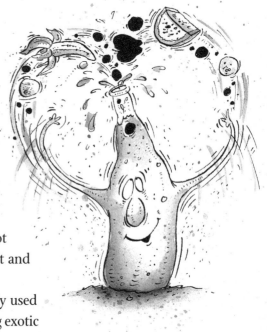

The Belgians seem to have the longest record of making fruit beers. They add cherries, raspberries, and other fruits to their spontaneously fermented lambic beers. The results are often tart and acidic with a dry, tannic fruit character. This approach is far different from the syrupy-sweet concoctions sometimes peddled here in the United States.

Many fruit beers express fruit in both aroma and flavor. A bit of fruit-derived color doesn't hurt, either. The real art is in not allowing the fruit to dominate the beer. In the best examples, malt and hop flavors are discernible in addition to the fruit.

Virtually any fruit can be used to flavor beer. I've successfully used cherries, raspberries, and blueberries. Others have made beer using exotic fruits—everything from huckleberries and marionberries to passion fruit and mangoes.

There are two schools of thought about how to add fruit to your beer. One school dumps the fruit into the hot wort shortly after the boil, allows it to steep half an hour or so, and removes it. The second school waits until primary fermentation is complete and adds the fruit to the secondary fermenter for one to four weeks.

Both systems have their advantages and risks; you'll just have to decide for yourself which way to do it.

Using either method, break up the fruit somewhat before you add it to the beer. For berries, freezing and then thawing can be an effective way to do this. Otherwise crush them, using a potato masher or spoon. Other fruits can be cut up by hand or chopped in a food processor.

As for quantities, one to two pounds of fruit per gallon of finished beer is usually about right. For milder fruits (e.g., peaches) or stronger-flavored beers (e.g., stouts), you'll want to be on the high end; for assertive fruits (e.g., raspberries) or lightly flavored beers (e.g., *helles*), aim for the lower end of the scale.

One final thought: if you have the patience to wait, fruit goes great in mead, too.

Bill Owens—Industry Pioneer

With more than forty years of homebrewing experience, Bill Owens is a man who exemplifies the phrase that appears at the beginning of this book: "Give a man a beer, and he wastes an hour; Teach a man to brew, and he wastes a lifetime."

PROFILE

Owens says that when he was a student in the 1950s, he bought cans of Premier malt extract that came with the following instructions: "Don't add this syrup to five gallons of water. Don't add hops and boil for one hour. Don't add yeast when cool. Don't ferment for two weeks. Don't add a teaspoon of sugar to each bottle. And don't drink the beer."

While his college beer achieved its primary purpose, it didn't capture his vocational attention, and he went on to pursue a career as a photographer. Later, while teaching sparsely attended photography classes, he noticed that the class in a room down the hall always drew a big crowd. It turned out to be a homebrewing class, and Owens decided to give it another try.

Soon he had learned the principles of all-grain brewing and had cobbled together his own home system. "It was hard enough just to get basic supplies like malt and hops," he says. "There was certainly no ready-made equipment available for grain brewing."

Not long after this, in the early 1980s, California legalized brewpubs and Owens decided to open one. When he went to his CPA for help raising money, the accountant relayed to him an old business plan and advised him to substitute "brewery" for "almond farm" throughout the document. "I did it and was able to raise the money, not because of the business plan, but because I was one of the few people who knew how to brew and how to put together a small brewery," he says.

Opened in 1983, Buffalo Bill's is one of the oldest brewpubs in America. In the early days, Owens relied heavily on his homebrewing experience and even his local homebrew supplier. "I used to get yeast from the homebrew shop," he says. "I'd buy a whole box of these little pouches and then sit there and cut every single one of them open so I could dump them in the wort."

In the beginning, he just made "beer," with no special style designation. Later he started making a beer called Amber, but he avoided calling it Pale Ale because that designation was being used by the nearby Sierra Nevada brewery.

In 1986, Owens created one of his most memorable beers, Pumpkin Ale. Made with real pumpkin in the mash, it brought him nationwide attention, including four lines of copy on the front page of the *Wall Street Journal.* Another of his brews, Alimony Ale, is reputed to be "America's most bitter beer."

In addition to running the brewpub, Owens founded two beer magazines: *American Brewer* and *Beer.* Both catered to the interests of the craftbrewing industry.

These days, his homebrewing continues and he makes three or four batches of beer a year, usually with his son. One recent batch was an imperial stout with an original gravity of 1.111. "It took thirty-three pounds of grain and two cans of extract for a ten-gallon batch," he says.

Despite his many years of brewing, Owens says he still finds joy in beer. "Over the years, you come to realize just how deep the culture of beer runs in man's soul," he says. "Basically, this is something that has been with us since we were all traveling in tribes."

HONEY OF A BEER

EARLY HOME- AND CRAFTBREWERS discovered that honey makes a great addition to beer. And, although most Americans think of honey as a single product, honey producers recognize many varieties (wildflower, orange blossom, buckwheat, and so on) with differing flavor characteristics. Brewing with honey can be as full of variation and adventure as you would like.

With honey, as with most other specialty ingredients, the trick is to express its character in both flavor and aroma while retaining a beer identity. Many have succeeded in striking this balance, and they use honey in a wide variety of styles from wheat beer to porter.

The general guideline is that honey should be 10 to 30 percent of the weight of your fermentable ingredients. So if you're making a beer with four pounds of extract and one pound of crystal malt, you'll want to add one-half to one-and-a-half pounds of honey.

When and how to add this honey is a matter of some discussion among brewers because of two issues. First, honey contains yeast and bacteria that are in a state of suspended animation because of the high sugar content. When the honey is diluted, these organisms can go to work and cause problems. So you need to pasteurize the honey, rather than adding it directly to your cold wort. On the other hand, boiling drives off volatile compounds that give honey its flavor and aroma. Thus, you don't want to heat the honey any more than is absolutely necessary for sanitizing purposes.

It's easiest to add the honey to the hot wort in the boil kettle a few minutes *after* you've turned off the fire. Let it sit for ten minutes, and then chill the wort as normal.

Another technique is to pasteurize the honey and add it to the fermenter after primary fermentation. This is supposed to improve retention of the volatile flavor and aroma compounds. Also, it lets you choose the pasteurization regimen precisely. Heating to 180 °F (82 °C) for five minutes will probably do it. Fifteen to twenty minutes at a cooler temp, say 160 °F (71 °C), will also probably work— especially if you're adding the pasteurized honey to fermented beer (which already contains bug-killing alcohol!).

No matter which route you choose, you're sure to be happy with the initial results. Then you can move on, exploring the different honeys, adding honey to different styles, or trying different addition techniques. You'll find many opportunities for fun in both the brewing and the consuming.

44

INFECT YOUR BEER FOR CLASSIC BELGIAN FLAVOR

AMONG PROFESSIONAL BREWERS, the Belgians are the quirkiest of the lot. The culture of farm-based brewing thrived in Belgium long after British and German brewers had moved on to industrial-scale production and worldwide distribution. As a result, brewing science in Belgium intentionally includes the use of organisms that brewers in other countries would never let near a beer.

The *lambic* beers of Belgium rely on brewing traditions that predate our understanding of yeast. To this day, brewers of these beers add no yeast to their cooled wort. Instead, they pump the beer into shallow open tanks in the rafters and allow the night air to waft in, bringing generous doses of wild yeast and bacteria.

The fermentation that follows involves a whole cast of organisms. Some, like brewers' yeast, ferment sugar to alcohol and carbon dioxide. Others prefer other metabolic pathways. They produce acetic acid, better known as vinegar, and lactic acid, a compound associated with sour milk. They also produce other organic compounds with leathery or animal-like characteristics. Individually, these flavors sound somewhat repulsive. But the lambic brewers have perfected their craft. They consistently make a tart, refreshing product.

You can find commercial lambics imported from Belgium at many liquor stores. Brands such as Cantillion and Boon display the traditional character of this style.

Lambics are not easy to produce, but plenty of homebrewers have given it a shot, with impressive results. Some set out intending to make a lambic beer. Others, I'm convinced, start their experimentation when an otherwise normal beer sours during fermentation.

At least five organisms participate in lambic production. Some of the better known examples are *Pediococcus damnosus* (so named because most brewers consider this organism to be a serious pest) and two species of the yeast genus *Brettanomyces: lambicus* and *bruxellensis.*

You can buy *Brettanomyces bruxellensis* from any homebrew retailer that handles Wyeast products, and *Pediococcus* cultures can also be found in homebrew channels these days. Add these cultures to the fermenter when primary fermentation with regular ale yeast is nearly complete, say ten days to two weeks after pitching. These supplemental organisms work slowly, so give them at least a month. Then you can sample the beer and bottle it.

True lambics are generally aged beers. You may find the character of a beer made with these supplemental organisms matures over many months or even several years. Set the bottles away somewhere cool, and try one every month or two. It will be fun to see how the flavors change and mature in the bottle.

45

A RELIGIOUS
EXPERIENCE WITH BELGIAN ALE

SINCE THE FALL OF ROME, MONASTERIES have provided shelter and sustenance for the weary throughout much of Europe. Beer they produced was part of that sustenance. In Belgium, the culture of monastic brewing remains strong today. Producing beer in their own facilities with the supervision and labor of monks, six abbeys in Belgium and the Netherlands define Trappist beer.

The word "Trappist" is protected by law for use by a limited number of producers. The six abbeys that use the name are Chimay, Rochefort, Orval, Westmalle, St. Sixtus (at Westvleteren), and Schaapskooi in the Netherlands.

Most Trappist brewers make two or three styles of beer that are generally quite fruity and complex and contain a good amount of alcohol. (By volume, alcohol ranges from 5.5 percent to just over 11 percent.) Not all of the Trappist beers produced can be neatly categorized, but two groups known as "double" and "triple" are frequently discussed.

The double is generally brown and has discernible chocolate, toasty, and nutlike malt flavors combined with a touch of sweetness. The alcohol content usually runs 6 percent and 8 percent by volume. Examples of this style often found in the United States include the Chimay Red (also called Premiere) and the Westmalle Dubbel.

The Trappist triples are somewhat stronger, although deceivingly pale in color. The highly fruity brews may display the aroma of ripe bananas, as well as some peach or clove character. They tend to be relatively dry, and the alcoholic strength is evident. The examples most commonly found in the United States are the Westmalle Tripel and the Chimay White Label (called Cinq Cents).

The key to making Trappist-style beer is to use the proper yeast, because it's the yeast that produces these beers' distinctive fruitiness. The easiest way to experiment is to buy a sample of Belgian yeast from your homebrew retailer. Another option is to harvest some yeast from the bottom of a Trappist beer bottle and use that. (For more on this, see Idea 46: Yeast Safari.)

Once you have the right yeast, the basic recipes for double and triple aren't hard to produce. Here are some examples to start with.

DOUBLE
6.6 pounds light malt extract
0.5 pound dark Crystal malt
0.25 pound chocolate malt
0.5 pound brown sugar in boil
4.5–5 alpha-acid units Saaz or Hallertau hops
     boiled for 60 minutes

TRIPLE
6 pounds light malt extract
2.5 pounds wheat malt extract
2 pounds Pilsener or two-row malt
0.5 pound candi sugar in boil
4.5–5 alpha-acid units Saaz or Hallertau hops boiled
     for 60 minutes

For both double and triple, add the crushed grains in a grain bag to cold water in your brewpot and begin heating. Remove the grains just before the water comes to a boil. Add remaining ingredients, and boil for 60 minutes.

TIME FOR A YEAST SAFARI

BY NOW, YOU'VE PROBABLY FIGURED out that there are lots of beer yeasts out there. It seems like a dozen or two varieties would be enough. But keep in mind there are thousands of breweries across Europe, and many use their own unique strains of yeast. Bottom line: the world of yeast is far greater than the prepackaged selection you'll find in the cooler at your homebrew store.

Now don't get me wrong; store-bought yeast has lots of advantages—convenience, purity, and reliability amongst them. But every now and then, it's fun to just break out of the mold and try something completely new.

New brewing yeast is pretty easy to come by. Plenty of imported beers, like homebrewed beers, are naturally carbonated and have yeast in the bottle. This means that every bottle-conditioned commercial beer, including Trappist ales, English bitters, and German *weizens,* includes a little present—a thin layer of yeast on the bottom. You can harvest this residue and use it in your own brews.

Some homebrew suppliers have yeast harvesting kits. But it's cheaper and almost as easy to start growing the yeast right away in its own bottle. Just add a cup of sterile wort and a fermentation lock to the bottle, and in a few days you should see some signs of fermentation. When this subsides, pour the contents of the bottle into a one- to two-quart yeast starter. Then start planning the beer you'll brew with the new yeast.

Here are some details on making sterile wort and yeast starters.

Sterile wort is nothing more than a very small batch of beer. To make one cup, you'll need a small saucepan with a cover, one-and-a-half cups of water, and two tablespoons of dry malt extract. If it's available, you could also add a small amount of yeast nutrient or yeast hulls—say an eighth of a teaspoon.

Mix the water, extract, and yeast nutrient in the saucepan and boil uncovered for about ten minutes. Cover loosely while boiling for another two minutes. Now turn off the fire, and place the lid securely on the top of the pot. If possible, set the pot in a shallow pool of cold water to help it cool faster. When the outside of the pot (and therefore the wort) has cooled to room temperature, the wort is ready to use. (Note: As an alternative to making sterile wort, you could harvest a cup of wort from the next batch of beer you make, and use that instead.)

Now, open the bottle where the yeast you want has been growing. Pour the beer into a glass, leaving all of the yeast and a small quantity of beer (about a quarter of an inch) in the bottom. Put a square of sanitized aluminum foil over the top, and go enjoy the beer. By the time you're done, the contents of the bottle should have warmed up to room temperature, and you can add the sterile wort. Using a clean, sanitized funnel, pour the sterile wort into the bottle. Now replace the sanitized foil, swirl and agitate the bottle aggressively for a few minutes, and set it aside to ferment.

If no fermentation occurs, the yeast may have been too old to be revived. You can try again with another bottle of the same beer or move on to another source. When you get one that works, transfer it to a larger starter before you pitch a whole five-gallon batch with the new yeast. Shoot for a one- to two-quart starter as the next step. If this begins to ferment within forty-eight hours of when you add the contents of the bottle, you should have enough yeast for five gallons.

If you find a yeast you like from a source like this, you may look into ways of storing a sample for later use. Some homebrew stores sell books and supplies that enable you to do this. If you really get into it, you could wind up with a nice collection of yeast samples that would be a valuable addition to your own brewing and a worthwhile resource for your homebrew club.

ARE YOU PORTER OR STOUT?

PORTER AND STOUT ARE WELL RECOGNIZED as the most commonly produced dark British-style ales. The two are closely related. Stout was originally just a strong porter, and for many years every brewery that made one made the other. These days, a lot of brewers make one style or the other, but few offer both.

Purists claim the distinction between porter and stout is clear, but you can't always tell it by tasting modern-day products. Roasted barley gives Guinness stout its coffeelike black-grain bitterness. As a result, some draw the dividing line between these two styles based on the use or exclusion of roasted barley. Others, citing the common ancestry of these two styles, insist such distinctions are strictly artificial.

You can brew two beers to help you explore and understand these styles. The stout follows the classic Guinness formulation. The porter recipe is the basic approach used by award-winning brewers.

Brew both beers using the same type of pale ale malt, the same extract, and the same yeast. When they're done, you'll have two beers that represent what experts feel is the difference between porter and stout. Taste and compare to see what you think.

For a fun group activity, taste these two beers along with five to ten commercial porters and stouts.

STOUT
Original gravity: 1.048
5 pounds pale malt extract syrup
1 pound pale ale malt
1 pound roasted barley

PORTER
Original gravity: 1.048
5 pounds pale malt extract syrup
1 pound pale ale malt
0.5 pound Crystal malt
0.25 pound chocolate malt
0.25 pound black malt

For both beers, the hops are 7 alpha-acid units of Galena, Eroica, or Centennial boiled for 60 to 70 minutes. Add 1/2 ounce of Willamette or Fuggles 15 minutes before the end.

48

TAKE A COOL SIP OF YOUR WARM BEER

ONCE YOU'VE INVESTED IN A SODA KEG for your beer, you may not always have room for it in your refrigerator. But even if the beer in the keg is warm, you can still enjoy a nice cool glass of brew.

Beer festivals and ball parks have long used a device known as a cold plate to chill warm beer as it's served. The cold plate is covered with ice. Beer flows through the channels inside, is chilled, and emerges cold and ready to drink. This principle can be applied to kegged homebrew to achieve your desired serving temperature.

To build your own cold plate, you'll need a spare serving hose with a keg connector on one end and a dispensing nozzle on the other. Halfway between the two ends, cut the hose. Now you have one piece of hose connected to a keg connector and another piece of hose with a dispensing nozzle.

Attach a copper coil in between the two cut hose ends. Buy about fifteen feet of copper tubing at your local hardware store. You'll probably want one-quarter or three-eighths-inch diameter, but check the size of hose you'll be attaching to make sure. At the hardware store, also pick up a couple of hose clamps.

Now coil the tubing. You can do this in a couple of ways, depending on how you plan to cool the coil. My jockey box is built around a little two-gallon picnic cooler that is taller than it is wide. So my tubing is coiled like a cylinder; each successive coil lies on top of the last one.

Folks who use a regular picnic cooler for this purpose wind the tubing in a flat spiral—each coil is just a bit larger than the last. This way, the cooling coil lies on the bottom of the cooler under all the ice. The rest of the cooler space can be used for food and more beer. No matter which pattern you use, remember to be gentle and careful with the tubing so that you bend it without crimping it!

You may want to permanently install the coil in the cooler. Mine is a dedicated unit that has holes for the coil to enter and exit. But you can make the coil portable, so it can be easily placed in the cooler when needed and then removed. This reduces the cost and improves the flexibility of your equipment.

When the tubing is coiled and the hoses are attached to either end, you're ready to add ice and beer. The beer should flow out of the keg into the hose and from there into the copper coil, where it is chilled. The cold beer exits the copper tube into the second half of the hose and runs through the dispensing nozzle into your glass.

Sounds like it's time for a nice cold beer!

One Determined Brewer Every now and then, the letters section of a brewing magazine chronicles the trials and tribulations of a beginning brewer. Some letters are instructive, others bizarre. This one just strikes me as funny, so I'll quote it directly:

I must laugh at your slogan "Relax, don't worry." With the first batch I brewed, I ruptured the water pipes in my wall using the jet spray bottle washer. I also couldn't get a siphon started from my carboy because I ran the racking tube through a rubber stopper and didn't allow air into the [carboy] bottle. I sucked out nearly half a gallon of beer before I figured it out. The best part is I kept rinsing my mouth out with overproof rum, and I was really ripped by the end of the bottling session. All in all the beer turned out great. When I bottled my fifth batch, the power went off and I finished by flashlight. Relax, I don't know, but I sure do love to brew now and I will brew forever.

[Signed] Anonymous (*Zymurgy* 1992)

87

THE BEER RAINBOW, OR, WHAT COLOR IS YOUR BEER?

BEER COLOR CAN BE HARD TO GET A HANDLE ON. The spectrum is described with words that don't always have a clear definition. The terms "pale," "straw," and "golden," taken alone, might mean about the same thing. But read a listing of beer descriptions, and you'll find each word designates a different color range.

When words aren't used, numbers substitute. In the United States, brewers use a system called "degrees SRM" (SRM is short for Standard Reference Method) to talk about beer color. Beers come in colors that range from 2 to more than 40 °SRM. But knowing that doesn't help you understand what a 14-°SRM beer should look like.

For the most part, homebrewers and beer drinkers have little to guide them in understanding beer color. That's why I've put together this chart. By using a few common beers as references, you can visualize the range of colors found in beer. At the same time, you can evaluate the color of some of your own beers.

To compare colors, pour the beers into identical glasses or cups. Clear, hard plastic cups will do nicely.

Now select four or five beers from the range of colors described. Most home-brewed beers fall in the gold to amber range, so be sure to select three standard beers from this area. I recommend Samuel Adams Boston Lager, Bass Ale, and Samuel Adams Doppelbock. Pour each standard beer into a cup or glass. To compare the beers, hold them in front of a brightly illuminated white sheet of paper. At this point, the relative differences in color should be evident.

Now, assess the color of some of your homebrews. Pour the homebrew into the same type of cup or glass you used for the standards. Now compare. It is more than likely the color of your homebrew will fall somewhere between two of the standards. To estimate the actual color rating for that brew, you'll have to decide about where in the range between the two standard beers your homebrew falls.

This approach to reading color is a fun activity for groups of brewers. When you open a beer to evaluate its color, you'll probably only need a few ounces of each one. The leftovers are fair game for anyone to drink or everyone to sample! So have fun—and don't forget to write down the color ratings for your homebrews. That will make it easier to remember the results in the morning.

CORRELATION OF SRM VALUES TO QUALITATIVE DESCRIPTIONS OF BEER COLOR

DESCRIPTION	SRM COLOR	EXAMPLE
Very pale	2–3	Budweiser (2)
Pale	3–4	Molson Export Ale (4.0)
Gold	5–6	
Amber (brownish-yellow)	6–9	Samuel Adams Boston Lager (7)
Deep amber/light copper	10–14	Bass Ale (9.8)
Copper (reddish-brown)	14–17	Samuel Adams Doppelbock (14–15)
Deep copper/light brown	17–18	Pete's Wicked Ale (18–19)
Brown	19–22	Salvator (21)
Dark brown	22–30	
Very dark brown	30–35	
Black	30+	
Black, opaque	40+	Most stouts

WOOD AGING YOUR BEER

ONLY IN THE PAST one hundred years have wooden fermenters and casks begun to disappear from breweries. Throughout Europe, you can still find wooden vessels of various types in use for fermenting and serving.

In the United States, brewers have moved more quickly away from wood to sanitary stainless-steel vessels. However, America's biggest brewer, Anheuser-Busch, still incorporates wood chips in its brewing process. And to add character to their beer, some smaller breweries have begun to experiment with new ways to use wood.

Aging beer in wood barrels holds a prominent place in the production of several alcoholic beverages. Vanilla and toasty traits in wines and whiskeys are often imparted by oak barrels. Makers of these fine beverages recognize and desire the flavor potential that can be extracted from wood.

In addition, they know that long periods of aging in wood produces other, more subtle changes. This occurs because the porosity of wood allows small amounts of air to interact with the beverage over the years. The slow oxidation that occurs mellows a fine Cabernet and contributes additional complexity to whiskeys. In the case of long-aged scotches, the character of the surrounding air—be it saturated with sea salt or bog peat—may be detected in the finished product.

Most beer lacks the alcohol content needed to fully extract wood flavor compounds. At the same time, beer's relatively short life span, compared with wine and whiskey, doesn't usually afford it the luxury of extended aging in wood.

Still, it's fun to experiment with wood aging by adding oak or other wood chips to your secondary fermenter. But first boil the chips for half an hour or more to ensure that they're well sanitized. Discard the water, and add the wood chips to the beer. Assuming the wood has not been previously used, you'll only need half a cup or so of chips to impart a discernible wood flavor to the beer. If you overdo it, you'll wind up with a product like my own batch 18—a beer that shall forever be known as the "pencil shavings beer."

If you really want to experiment, try toasting some of the wood chips over a charcoal fire to achieve some of the toasted character of Chardonnay wine. When you hit that magic combination of recipe, wood, and process, don't forget to share the results with your fellow brewers.

Dryer Hopping If you grow your own hops, one question you'll face is how to dry them after they've been harvested. People have bought or invented a variety of devices for this purpose, employing light bulbs, hair dryers, and home food dehydrators along the way. But the most innovative idea I have heard of was the fellow who used a clothes dryer to dry the hops. He  told me he just zipped the hops into one of those net bags women use for drying nylons and threw them into the dryer on low heat for about an hour. Assuming there would be a residual smell in the dryer, I was surprised that anyone would do this. "How did the next batch of clothes smell?" I asked.

"I don't know," he said, "I used a dryer down at the local laundromat."

BREAK YOUR VACUUM

IF YOU USE GLASS CARBOYS for fermentation, you've probably become accustomed to the splashing and shaking you go through every time you try to clean one. Getting water into them isn't so bad—but getting it out can be a real mess. And if that water is spiked with chlorine or some other cleaning agent, the resulting shower can go in your eyes, ruin your clothes, or pit nearby stainless-steel items.

You don't have to endure this mess. All it takes is one little piece of plastic tubing inserted into the inverted carboy. It allows air to come in while the water and other stuff comes out, resulting in a faster and neater flow.

If you lose your piece of tubing, you have one other option. Swirl the inverted carboy so all the water spins around inside. This will create a vortex up the middle of the carboy. Air comes in up the vortex; water runs out around the edges. The flow becomes fast and neat.

52

DRY HOP WITH CHILI PEPPERS

ONE OF THE NICEST CHILI PEPPER beers I ever tasted was also one of the easiest to make. Ray Dean at the Railroad Brewery in Anchorage, Alaska, makes a Steel Rail Chili Ale that is dry hopped with Anaheim chilies in the fermenter and then taste-tested until ready. His beer has a great pepper aroma, but there's not much heat or pepper character in the flavor. As a result, it's nicely balanced and very drinkable. It would be great with food of any kind.

Give this idea a try next time you make a beer that might go well with chili peppers—anything from Pilsener to *maibock* and bitter to barley wine. Add a pepper or two to the secondary fermenter. Sample the beer every few days until the pepper character is discernible in both the flavor and aroma. When you've got something you like, simply rack, bottle, and enjoy.

SPECIAL SPIKED ALE THE EASY WAY

SPICED BEERS ARE FUN TO EXPERIMENT WITH, but you don't always want five gallons of the finished product. Instead, you can season just part of a batch.

A few years ago, I made an award-winning spiced *helles* practically one bottle at a time. The spices came premixed in a carton and were called Aspen Mulling Spices, which includes nutmeg, cinnamon, annatto, lemon, and clove. When the basic helles beer was finished, I took a sample in a measuring cup and started adding the spice mix. A quarter teaspoon was just barely detectable, so I put in a quarter teaspoon more. That had a nice spice flavor and allowed the beer flavors to come through as well. Just to be sure, I added another quarter teaspoon and found, as I expected, that the result was overwhelmingly "mulled" with not enough apparent beer flavor.

Based on these results, I racked six bottles worth of beer into a clean gallon jug and then added the proper proportion of the spice mixture. This went into bottles. Once carbonated, the resulting beer gave just what I was looking for: a pleasant expression of spice on a background of pale malt flavor.

Using this same technique, you can spice a portion of your next brew. You can buy ready-made mixes or create your own combinations of spices. Simply mix the powdered spices together into a uniform blend, and then use the blend to spike your beer to taste.

If you were to do this for every beer you made, you'd soon have nice collection of spiced beers to taste and enjoy. Better yet, if a whole club did this for a couple of months, the resulting beers would make for an excellent herb-and-spice beer meeting.

PROGRESSIVE BEER DINNER

BEER AND FOOD ARE NATURAL COMPANIONS, of course. And it turns out that many good brewers are also talented chefs. Thinking about this, the phrase "total creative control" comes to mind. Each brewer/chef is given a course and decides what to make and how to make it. Then he or she decides what beer to serve with the food and makes that too!

This requires some advance planning if you want to make the beer specifically for the food. No doubt the average procrastinator will just make food that goes with a beer already on hand. In any case, it should be quite a feast when everything is sampled in the course of an evening. If the participants live in the same area and responsible transportation can be arranged, you might do each course at a different house. Or just bring all the food and beer to a single location, and enjoy a long evening of beery feast and fun.

MAKE A NAME FOR YOUR BEER

I ALWAYS WONDERED HOW CREATIVE types came up with the great names they give their beers. You know—things like Dick's Elixir, Pudgy McBuck's Cocoa Porter, Freemont Plopper Pilsener, and Rocky Raccoon's Crystal Honey Lager. Recently, fellow Chicago Beer Society member Randy Mosher showed me a technique he sometimes uses to generate names.

The technique requires 3-by-5 cards or other small pieces of paper. Write one word or description on each card, and then start shuffling. As you shuffle, you discover combinations that sound good together. Along the way, you might add a new word or phrase to complete a partial name, and viola!—you have the perfect name for your latest creation.

This naming game could be fun to try either alone or with a group. First, have a beer to get the creative juices flowing. Now, create three groups of cards as follows:

GROUP A

Names or namelike adjectives—Pick some funny names for people or places, like "Cornelius Fogg," "North Zulch," or "Tip Roaster." Also pick a few adjectives that usually end with ous, like "delicious," "fallacious," or "mischievous."

GROUP B

Nouns or noun phrases—Words like "steamboat," "eraserhead," or "alleycat" might be good. You can also throw in some modified nouns like "ghost ship," "harvest moon," or "broken arrow."

GROUP C:

Words for beer—This can include style names (porter, Pilsener), synonyms like "grog" or "potion," and maybe some compound names like "pungent lambic" or "high-test hock."

If you are picking a name for a specific beer, the words you select for group C will be easy; you'll want them to say what kind of beer it really is. As for groups A and B, concentrate on a specific theme—rock and roll, space travel, American literature . . . anything goes!

Pick a card from group A and place it in front of you. Now look through the group B cards and pick one you like. Now, proceed to group C. Mix and match. Throw all the cards up in the air, and pick them up off the floor at random. Soon, I'm sure, you'll find a fun and fitting name for your latest beer.

If a group is doing this, split into three teams to make up words for each category. Write the words on large cards big enough for everyone in the room to see. When it comes time to make up names, each team takes a card to the front of the room and presents its portion. You can put the cards on a bulletin board or just have people hold them up in order. In any case, everyone should be able to see the cards and read the new name. Mix and match. Throw the cards in the air and pick them up off the floor at random. Have fun!

GROW YOUR OWN HOPS

HOPS ARE NOT ONLY ESSENTIAL TO BEER, but they're also an attractive peren-nial vine. They are easy to plant and care for, and when fall comes, you can harvest them for use in your first brew of the season.

If you have the space, you can build your own "hop yard," complete with poles and wires, the way the pros do it. But even a tiny yard or a large patio planter will support one or two plants.

Some homebrew shops—especially those that also sell gardening supplies—sell hop rhizomes in the spring. A rhizome is a specialized part of the plant that gives rise to new growth each spring. Drop one in your garden by the beginning of May, and it will be growing before you know it.

The key to growing hops isn't square footage of yard space, but vertical feet of climbing room. The one little plant I put in a few years ago now climbs more than twenty feet up my back patio each year. If you don't have room for them to grow that high, give them room to spread horizontally. I rig a T-shaped configuration of twine over my hops each year, with the top of the T set at about eighteen feet. The hops grow up and then grab on to the horizontal twine and spread along it. Good places to grow your hops include next to your house or garage or along a fence or border.

Remember these two things about growing hops. First, the finished hops will be a relatively unknown quantity. If you're careful, you'll be able to tell what variety you have, but you still won't know the alpha-acid content. So, it may be hard to know how much of your hops to add for a particular type of beer. For this reason, I prefer to grow aroma hop varieties, like Cascade, that can be used in the finish of the beer based on weight rather than for their bittering properties.

The other thing is that hops produce quite a lot of vegetation. A single plant can put out several vines, and each grows at an amazing rate. I know a brewer who planted just half a dozen plants beside his garage. All the vines met at the top of the T and became hopelessly tangled. He had a tough time harvesting and really couldn't tell which variety was which. My advice is to stick with one variety—and separate them if you plant more than one plant.

When fall comes, it's time to harvest. If the hops climbed on twine, simply cut both twine and vine at bottom and top. The whole thing drops to the ground, where it's easier to pull off the hop cones. Fresh cones are mostly water, so use them within a few days or dry them for storage. You can dry hops at very low heat (100 °F [38 °C]) in the oven or in a food dehydrator and store them in the freezer for several months before use.

Another fun thing to do with your hops is to use the vines as decoration at a beer or homebrew event. Drape them around the door or down the middle of the table, or hang them over the podium. It adds a wonderful authentic touch for your fall events.

57

CONSORT WITH THE DEVIL: HOLD A HOP FESTIVAL

IN SOME HOP-GROWING REGIONS of Europe, a character known as the hop devil appears at the annual harvest festival. Although the exact origins of this are little known, the details are easy to imagine. The hop devil is a mischievous clown who represents all the obstacles to a successful hop harvest: drought, disease, bugs, and strong winds, among others. During the harvest festival, someone dressed as the hop devil dances through the crowd spilling beers, stealing kisses, and generally making a nuisance of himself.

When festivalgoers have had enough, the chase is on. Once they catch the devil, they can bind him to a tree with hop vines as penance (hop vines are very rough and spiny) or simply incarcerate him in a convenient spot until the festival has come to an end. But no matter how he's dealt with, this devil is kept amply supplied with good beer to ensure his good graces for the following year.

Many homebrew clubs stage an annual picnic that features homebrew, home cooking, and fun for the whole family. If this event is held in the fall, it can incorporate elements of the hop harvest festival. In addition to witnessing an appearance by the hop devil, you can enjoy a beer produced from the first hops harvested that year or make a hop harvest beer at the picnic. (See Idea 59: Brew in the Woods.) Have each member bring a small sample of their favorite hops, or have people bring their homegrown hops to add. The resulting beer—offered at your next monthly meeting—will be a pleasant reminder of the good time had by all.

58

HAVE A MEETING WITH STYLE

ONCE YOU START BREWING, you begin to appreciate how many different types of beer there are in the world. Some brewers settle on one or two favorites, while most have a broader interest in styles. A great way to expand and enhance everyone's knowledge of beer styles is to pick one style as the meeting's focus .

Exactly what you do at a style meeting depends on the available resources and the nature of your group. The Chicago Beer Society did style meetings for a couple of years, and each one generally had three components: a presentation, tasting of commercial beers, and tasting of homebrewed beers.

The presentation doesn't have to be a big deal, and the person making the presentation doesn't have to be an expert. But he or she should make an effort to learn as much as possible in preparation for the presentation.

These days, a ton of information is available about most beer styles, including data about commercial examples and directions for brewing a proper example. (If you need help, call the Association of Brewers in Boulder, Colorado, and ask for a catalog of the books they publish.) Armed with a couple of good books, almost anyone can pull together a nice talk on a specific style. If the speaker happens to love the style, happens to have traveled to its native land, so much the better.

For commercial examples to taste, refer to published sources to identify good models and bring four to six of them to the event. For homebrewed contributions, get people to brew beers that illustrate specific elements of the style. For pale ales, offer the same beer two ways: with and without dry hops. If either porter or stout is the topic, have someone brew the two examples in Idea 47: Are You Porter or Stout? For Pilsener, ask two brewers to follow identical recipes except for a change in the base malt. If there are plenty of volunteer brewers, have them brew examples of the style's subcategories—for instance, sweet stout, oatmeal stout, foreign stout, and dry stout.

BREW IN THE WOODS

FOR MUCH OF ITS HISTORY, BREWING has been an outdoor activity. Only with the coming of the industrial age have we tamed it and brought it inside. To reproduce the spirit (and fun) of the olden days and ways, stage an outdoor brew-in.

Chicago Beer Society beer geeks have done several backyard brews. For years we've talked about (but never made good on) the idea of a homebrew camp-out—one where the consumption of good homebrew would be accented by the production of an atavistic brew. There's something undeniably wonderful about the idea of a weekend in the woods with nothing but a dozen smiling beer geeks and a lot of homebrew in various stages of completion.

Brewing outdoors presents certain challenges, but nothing insurmountable. For some folks, backyard brewing is nothing new—they brew in the yard on a regular basis using propane burners and garden hoses. But if you don't normally brew outdoors, a backyard shakedown brew is a good first step before you take your brewpots into wilder and less hospitable surroundings.

Of course, the backyard affords you certain luxuries more primitive settings deny—first and foremost, the ability to run in the house to get anything you may have forgotten.

When you do venture away from home, you can use various heat sources, from the reliable propane burner (make sure you have a full tank of propane!) to the most basic of roaring fires.

Most campsites provide potable water you can use for the brew itself. You face a greater challenge when it comes time to chill your wort. One dreams of nestling the pot in a frigid stream, but this isn't always an option. And even if your campsite's water source is fitted with garden hose threads, other campers may not be too happy if you monopolize it with your wort chiller. Creativity may be in order.

Watch out for sunlight, too. Beers become skunky after brief exposure to direct sunlight. Be sure to keep your glass carboys covered or in the shade. And speaking of carboys, unless you plan a very long camping trip, they're likely to be full of actively fermenting beer during your trip home. A nice solid blowoff system will probably be in order. Also, plan the explanation you'll offer if you're stopped for a traffic violation with huge carboys of fermenting beer in your back seat!

Finally, be spontaneous. You never know what tasty herb or ripe fruit you might find growing adjacent to your campsite. Add it to the pot to produce a beer that will bring back memories of the trip.

STUNTED GROWTH: THE MAGIC OF MALT

WE USE THE WORD "MALT" SO OFTEN when talking about beer that we sometimes have to remind ourselves that what we're talking about malted barley. Barley in its raw form looks a lot like the malted product, but otherwise it's vastly different.

From the barley's point of view, malting is a cruel process. After all, barley is a seed. Its purpose in life is to sprout and grow so it will one day be a mature barley plant with more seeds of its own. But brewers have long had other plans for barley.

When barley germinates, roots shoot out one end, and the tiny plant begins to grow from there toward the other end of the kernel. But before this shoot reaches the other end, the maltster throws the kernel into a giant oven to be dried and toasted. The roots wither and fall off, the shoot dries into a state of suspended animation, and the whole kernel enters a stable, dormant phase. This allows malt to be stored for long periods before it's used.

Germination is necessary to convert raw barley into the commodity needed by brewers. During malting, much of the kernel softens as the starch is converted into a form that will be accessible during brewing. In addition, malting awakens the enzymes needed for brewing and then suspends their progress so they'll be ready for action in the mash.

At least once, every brewer should cut open a piece of malt to see what's inside. If you can, compare it with raw barley so you can see what a difference malting has made. Here's the twenty-five-cent tour of a malt kernel.

The kernel has two ends. The wider, blunter end is where the action begins. Three to five rootlets emerge here early in the malting process and grow to be one to two inches long. If you look closely, you can see where they've broken off.

Each kernel has a deep crease or fold that runs lengthwise. Using a razor blade, cut the grain in half down this fold. Inside, look for two things. First, notice that the inside is mostly white and has a chalky or powdery appearance. This is starch that has been modified during malting. Now look up toward the pointy end of the kernel. You may see a small portion of the starch mass that is off-white and smooth or pearly looking. This is unmodified starch. These days most malts are very well modified, but some German Pilsener malts may still show a bit of hard, unmodified starch. This material is so hard and impervious to water that it will not be accessible during mashing. Its starch (and therefore sugar) is lost during the brewing process.

Finally, look for the tiny malt plant that grew during malting. It grows up the back of the kernel—opposite the crease you used as a guide when you cut the grain open. You'll find the plant between the starch and the husk; it may have been cut in half the long way when you cut the grain. It usually doesn't look like much—just a tan, withered strip that runs nearly the entire length of the kernel. If you don't see it in the first grain you cut, cut a few others until you get a good view.

BRING YOUR BUDDIES TO A BREW-A-THON

YOU KNOW ABOUT MARATHONS and maybe even dance-a-thons, so what is a brew-a-thon? A nonstop day of brewing, what else?

The Great Northern Brewers Club in Anchorage, Alaska, does this as an annual event. They start brewing at 8 A.M. and don't stop until about 11 P.M. that night. Usually they keep eight to ten brews bubbling at a time. They produce hundreds of gallons of beer over the course of the day.

Two unique elements make their brew-a-thon special. First, the local homebrew store offers a 20 percent discount on ingredients used in brew-a-thon beers. That helps to encourage participation among brewers of all stripes. Second, each of the two-person teams is supposed to include a novice brewer, so the event introduces new brewers to the hobby. They'll get a chance to see how beer is brewed, to meet other homebrewers, and to sample homebrew that's offered at the event.

In the Great Northern Brewers program, extract brews are produced in three-hour shifts to maximize output. Usually one club member also brings along an all-grain setup for demonstration purposes. It's a great way to learn more about brewing and your fellow brewers, no matter how much beer you've made.

Best of all, you can plan a big homebrew picnic or party about six weeks after the brew-a-thon so everyone can sample the beers and relive the fun of the brewing day.

Why not plan your club's brew-a-thon for two months from today?

SOUR MASH BEER

IF YOU'VE EVER LOOKED AT A BOTTLE of bourbon, you've probably noted the words "sour mash" on the label. Brewers sometimes use a sour mash as well, and it can make for an interesting beer.

The first steps in making whiskey are similar to those for making beer. Raw and malted grains are crushed and mixed with hot water to form a mash in which starch can be converted to sugar. For whiskey, the wort that's drawn off is fermented immediately without being boiled. After fermentation, whiskey-makers distill the resulting "beer" to produce the raw whiskey that will be aged before distribution. (By the way, home distillation is illegal in the United States, and it can also be quite dangerous. Few things are more explosive than alcohol vapor.)

The distinctions among different types of whiskey are in the grains used. Scotch, like beer, is made from barley malt. Bourbon is made primarily from corn, but some barley is used to aid conversion, and some wheat or rye is usually added as well. In whiskey-making as in the making of sourdough bread, some of the sour mash is held back and added to the next batch, creating continuity between batches.

The same Kentucky craftsmen who made whiskey also used to make some beer. They used a sour-mash process of a slightly different type, one that makes a little more sense to beer-makers.

Lactic-acid bacteria are naturally present in grain, so any mixture of grain and hot water will start to sour after a few hours. If a mash is left sitting overnight in an insulated container, a distinctly sour mash will result.

Interesting beers can be made using sour mash, as past Homebrewer of the Year Ray Spangler has demonstrated. Spangler lives in Erlanger, Kentucky, just across the river from Cincinnati. Living in this area, he has had a unique opportunity to research sour-mash beers.

At the 1991 National Homebrewers Conference, Spangler presented the results of his research. He suggested letting the mash rest eighteen to twenty-four hours in an insulated mash tun (that is, a picnic cooler). Before sparging, remove any scum that may have formed on the top of the mash.

Although Spangler talks about initial mash temperatures as high as 167 °F (75 °C), you could probably get away with something like 158 °F (70 °C). After the sparge, treat the wort as you would normally.

Here is a recipe for Kentucky Common Beer, adapted from Spangler's original all-grain version.

KENTUCKY COMMON BEER (makes 5 gallons)
2 pounds pale or two-row malt
1 pound dark (50 °L or greater) Crystal malt
3 ounces chocolate or black patent malt

Mix these crushed grains together with 1 gallon of 173-°F (78-°C) water in a small insulated cooler. Stir well to mix and then again every 15 minutes for the first 90 minutes. Otherwise, keep covered. After 90 minutes, cover and let stand about 24 hours. Skim off any scum, and then lauter the grains as normal.

Now add the following:

3.3 pounds wheat malt extract syrup or 3 pounds dry wheat malt extract
enough water to bring the total volume to 5 gallons
4 alpha-acid units hops boiled for 60–90 minutes

When the boil is complete, cool and ferment as normal. The finished beer will have a unique lactic flavor that may vary from soft to assertive.

By the way, this technique has been used by German brewers for many years to help acidify their mashes. German purity laws prohibit the addition of acid to the mash, so brewers simply add a small portion of soured mash to achieve the same purpose.

Jim Parker—This Is Fun!

Jim Parker brewed his first beer in 1987 using a seven-barrel brewpub setup. At the time he was a feature writer for the *Contra Costa Times* in Walnut Creek, California. "The editor picked me to do a story on the local brewpub, because she figured I drank more beer than anyone else on the feature staff," he says.

After he interviewed Greg Jones at Devil Mountain brewpub about the brewing process, Parker asked Jones if he could watch him brew sometime. "Jones said no," recalls Parker. "He said I couldn't watch— but I could help."

PROFILE

The next day, Parker showed up in old clothes and boots and participated in what would be the first of many brews. By the end of the day, he was captivated. "I had seen my brother make beer from extract in college," he says, "but I thought that was pretty boring. Brewing with grain was fun."

Over the next several months, Jones tutored Parker in beer-making, providing grain, hops, and yeast from the brewpub. "I would make the beer and bring it in, and he would tell me what I had done wrong," says Parker. "On the fourth try, I got the amber beer right and he let me move on to making a stout."

Not long after this, Parker decided he needed to make brewing a bigger part of his life. He proceeded to teach homebrew classes and started writing one of the first weekly beer columns in the United States. Once immersed in the beer culture, he moved to Colorado where he started the *Rocky Mountain Brews* newspaper, and opened the Mountain Tap tavern in Fort Collins. "The Mountain Tap was listed as one of the ten best beer bars in America by *Barleycorn* magazine," he relates. Although he didn't homebrew much during this time, he eventually found himself back at the brew kettle.

For two years, he was head brewer at the ten-barrel Dimmer's brewpub in Fort Collins. There he created beers such as Blonde Bomber, inspired by an old girlfriend, and Old Bald Fart.

"I kind of like hops," he says of these beers. Old Bald Fart included twenty-three pounds of hops—an amount equal to putting 5.5 ounces of hops in five gallons of homebrew.

Other beers he made there include a fruit beer based on plums and a wheat beer using wheat toasted in the brewpub's oven. "I didn't just want to make beers like those other people were making," he says. "I wanted to be a little creative."

When Dimmer's closed, he took a job at the Association of Brewers and eventually wound up being appointed as director of the American Homebrewers Association.

Now that he is homebrewing again, the innovation continues. "Last weekend I was doing a porter and wound up throwing in some flaked rye and malt toasted in the oven," he says. "I also did a peat-smoked porter not long ago that I liked."

Mentioning ingredients like quinoa and agave, he says he appreciates the opportunity to be really creative in his brewing again. One upcoming project is the challenge of brewing a great malt liquor. "They have a malt liquor category at the Dixie Cup homebrew competition in Houston, so I just have to see if I can make one."

"The reason I got involved with beer to begin with is because it's fun," Parker says. "If I can't make strange beers and use weird ingredients, what's the use of brewing at all?"

CARAMELIZE YOUR WORT FOR SPECIAL FLAVOR

FLAVOR AND COLOR GO HAND IN HAND in brewing. When we add color to the beer, we usually add some new flavors as well. Mind you, a pale beer can be very flavorful, but the darker colors bring different flavor dimensions to the brew.

When adding color to our beer, we turn to dark malts. From biscuit to black and Crystal to chocolate, maltsters provide a wide array of products to choose from.

But there's another way to add color and flavor, something that can't quite be duplicated in any other way: caramelization. This occurs when sugars are heated or scorched during the boil. It happens in most flame-fired kettles to a certain extent, but you can accentuate the effect by using several different techniques.

The most common method of caramelization is the long boil. Some all-grain brewers do this as a matter of course, because their mash yields far more runoff than they need. When wort is boiled more than two hours, the caramelization effect begins to become noticeable. It is also more pronounced when the wort is higher in gravity.

A second technique is to take a small pan of wort (perhaps the first runnings from a mash) and boil it aggressively. I have a rather thin aluminum saucepan I sometimes use for this purpose. In two hours, I can reduce two quarts of wort down to about half a quart and achieve a good deal of caramelization as well. I add this wort back to the main boil just before cooling.

Finally, some brewers tell me they actually heat their empty kettles. When the first wort comes in contact with the hot kettle, some of the sugar is instantly caramelized. Just be careful: the arrival of that first wort on the hot kettle bottom will produce a lot of steam, and super-hot wort may splatter out.

These techniques can be used to make virtually any type of beer. It is recommended in the making of Scotch and Scottish ales, and it can be used for other styles such as brown ale, porter, and even *bock*.

A PALE IMITATOR

THE PALE BEERS MADE BY AMERICAN brewers have long included substantial quantities of raw grains. Today, the leading American mass-market beers are made from a grist that is about 30 percent corn or rice. In some budget brands, these raw grains may equal nearly 50 percent of the grist weight.

Because most of us grew up drinking these beers, eventually many homebrewers want to try to make the same thing. In fact, it's fun to see if you can copy—or perhaps improve on—a beer that millions drink every day.

Because corn and rice have not been malted like the barley brewers commonly use, special processing is required to convert their starch to sugar. The general approach is to boil the grain with water for some time and then to combine the resulting gruel with barley malt to create a mixed-grain mash. From here on, the process continues like it would for any other all-grain brew.

If you'd like to give this a try, here's a recipe and procedure for a nice pale beer I made a few years ago. It uses good-quality hops to provide a crisp bitterness and a wonderful hop flavor and aroma.

MILLER'S ENVY (makes 5 gallons)
6 pounds two-row or Pilsener malt
2.5 pounds table rice
2 ounces Crystal, Liberty, Mt. Hood, or Saaz hops

Crush the malt into one container. Using your grain mill, grind the rice into small pieces in a separate container. A couple of passes may be needed to break the grains into small pieces.

Combine the rice and 1/2 pound of the malt with 1.5 gallons of cold water. Heat, stirring occasionally. When the temperature reaches 175 °F (79 °C), lower the heat and hold at this temperature about 10 minutes. During the 10-minute rest, start the barley mash by mixing the remaining malt and 1 tablespoon of gypsum with 1.75 gallons of 135-°F (57-°C) water. Mix well and let rest.

After the rice has completed its 10-minute rest, turn the heat up again and bring the pot to a boil. Boil 20 to 30 minutes, stirring frequently to prevent scorching. Add more water if the mixture becomes stiff.

At the end of the rice boil, cut the heat and begin transferring the rice mixture to the barley mash. Stir the two together and check the mash temperature. If it's below 152 °F (67 °C) or above 158 °F (70 °C), heat or cool the mash to attain this range. Mash 45 to 60 minutes and run off following your normal mash procedures.

In the boil pot, add the hops as follows:

HOP ADDITIONS

MINUTES BEFORE END OF BOIL	AMOUNT OF HOPS (ounces)
90	0.25
45	0.25
20	0.5
10	0.5
0	0.5

This recipe was brewed originally as a lager, but I'm sure it will make a great-tasting ale as well.

HAVE BEER, WILL TRAVEL

SO YOU BOUGHT SOME SODA KEGS, and you love the fact you don't have to bottle anymore. Now all you need is a way to take your show on the road.

For years now, fellow homebrewer Randy Mosher and I have talked about making a beer backpack. Here's the plan: get a backpack frame that will support a three-gallon soda keg and a two-and-a-half-pound carbon dioxide gas bottle. Fashion an attachment system for these items so the backpack can be loaded up, put on, and hauled around. Of course, you'll have to rig a long dispensing tube so the wearer can dole out beer as he or she walks around. We always thought it would be fun to hook the dispensing head to a triggered wand of some sort that would allow for dispensing brew to throngs of thirsty homebrewers.

A similar concept is built around a two-wheeled golf bag carrier. Because of the wheels, this system could accommodate a five-gallon soda keg and a regular-sized carbon dioxide bottle. You might even decide to hook up a little jockey box on this rig so the beer would always be served cool, even after you had dragged it around eighteen holes or half a mile up the trail to your favorite picnic site.

HERE'S AIR IN YOUR BEER

ONE IMPORTANT STEP in making beer is aeration of the cool wort before the yeast is pitched. Normally, air is not a good thing for beer—but this is the one time it's needed. The yeast needs some oxygen during the early part of fermentation so it can grow and reproduce. Thus, air at this point contributes to a normal, healthy fermentation.

Most homebrewers aerate their wort just by splashing it as it goes into the fermenter. But sometimes this isn't enough. Some yeast strains need more oxygen than others. Also, higher-gravity worts need more aggressive aeration to achieve the proper levels of dissolved oxygen.

You can buy oxygenator systems at many homebrew stores, but bottles of oxygen can get expensive. Another alternative is to use an aquarium pump to build your own little aeration system. Here's what you'll need: an aquarium air pump, an aeration stone (beer carbonation stone is ideal), a disposable sterile filter (from a surplus store), and plastic tubing (four to five feet).

Use the plastic tubing to connect all the elements so air flows from the aquarium pump to the sterile filter and then to the carbonating stone. You may want to use some drilled stoppers to help attach the filter.

When this is all rigged, sanitize the carbonating stone and about three feet of tubing in bleach or iodine. Then rack your cool wort into the fermenter, and drop the stone into the wort. Turn on the pump and watch the bubble show. Ten minutes should do the trick, but don't walk off and leave it running unattended the first few times you use it. The bubbles might foam out of the fermenter, making a big mess for you to clean up on your return!

When you're through aerating, pitch your yeast, and don't forget to carefully clean and sanitize the aeration stone.

A COZY KEG IS A COOL KEG

BEER IN A KEG IS BEER THAT'S BEGGING to go to a party, a picnic, or just your next homebrew club event. But once you take the keg out of the refrigerator, the beer will start to warm up, and eventually it will be too warm to enjoy.

You can help your beer keep cool with a keg cozy. This is an insulated jacket that goes around the keg, acting like a custom-fitted cooler. You can buy one, of course, but a homemade one can carry your own custom design—and it'll probably be a lot cheaper.

Here's the basic plan: Soda kegs are twenty-eight inches in circumference. The five-gallon ones are about twenty-five inches tall; the three-gallon ones, about sixteen inches. All you need to make a keg cozy is two pieces of cloth cut to the appropriate dimensions and some insulating material to go in between. The dense foam pads sold for camping or exercising are excellent for insulation. Sew the two cloth panels together with the pad in between. Then sew the ends together to form a tube you can fit over your keg. If you have a talented tailor or seamstress at your disposal, you might use a sturdy zipper instead. You could also consider installing a drawstring or some cinch straps to help keep the cozy firmly in place. And don't forget to add some personal touches to the outside of the cozy, be they polka-dotted, tie-dyed, or embroidered.

WELCOME LIFE WITH MAJORITY ALE

BREWING FAMILIES IN ENGLAND sometimes celebrate the birth of an heir by brewing a special strong ale called Majority Ale. These beers are brewed around the time of the birth and then stashed away. When the child reaches the age of majority, achieving manhood (or the modern equivalent, legal drinking age), the special ale is ceremoniously served.

Most beers are well past their prime after they've aged for two decades. But if you have a new arrival, you can still make a special brew to mark the occasion. As a variation on tradition, you might open one bottle each year around the time of the child's birthday as a suitable reward for another year of diligent parenting. If you bottle a five-gallon batch in twenty-two-ounce bottles, you should have enough to try a bottle each year and still have six or eight left over for the final celebration.

Both alcohol and the color-producing substances called melanoidins improve a beer's chances of aging well. Thus, our majority ale will be both strong and black, borrowing heavily from the traditions of Russian imperial stout. Use a good bit of grain in this beer to enhance flavor and complexity. All-grain brewers, however, should supplement the basic recipe with malt extract to get the desired strength.

This recipe allows for many variations. Write it down and keep it in a safe place. You'll want to revisit the details years from now as you enjoy the results!

A SCORE PLUS ONE ALE (makes 5 gallons)
Target original gravity: 1.120
1 pound pale ale malt
1 pound dark Crystal malt (80–120 °L)
1 pound specialty malt of your choice (aromatic, biscuit, victory, and so on)
0.5 pound roast barley

Supplement this with eleven pounds of dry malt extract or thirteen pounds of extract syrup, mixing several different brands to increase the complexity of the beer. I recommend at least three pounds of dark extract; the rest can be amber or pale. Use unhopped extracts in all cases. If you're a pound or a pound and a half short of the total and don't want to use just part of a package of extract, make up the difference with honey or brown sugar.

HOPS

15–20 alpha-acid units of bittering hops (Select Galena, Chinook, or another high-alpha acid variety for this purpose.)

5 ounces aroma-type hops (Select 1-ounce packages to be added at 30 minutes, 20 minutes, 15 minutes, 10 minutes, and 5 minutes. Mix and match varieties as you wish.)

28 grams dry ale yeast (That's four packages in most cases, or repitch yeast from a previous batch of beer.)

Mini-mash the grains, or soak them in 3 gallons of water at 150 °F (65 °C) for about an hour before removing grains with a strainer. To the resulting wort, add the extract and the bittering hops and bring to a boil. After 45 to 60 minutes of boiling, start adding the aroma hops. Put in 1 ounce at each of the following times before the end of the boil: 30 minutes, 20 minutes, 15 minutes, 10 minutes, and 5 minutes.

At the end of the boil, chill as usual. Take extra care to aerate the wort well before pitching the yeast. After primary, or the first week to ten days of fermentation, transfer this beer to a secondary fermenter. It can probably stay there for many months before being bottled. After bottling, store it in a cool place, preferably at a temperature less than 60 °F (15 °C). Storage under lock and key is recommended during the mid- to late-teenage years!

69

CURE THE BITTERNESS BLUES

AFTER YOU'VE BREWED A COUPLE OF batches of beer, you start to experiment. A little more of this, a little less of that—and eventually, you're making up your own recipes from scratch.

One of the most important elements of recipe formulation is achieving the right level of bitterness. Throughout this book, we talk in terms of AAUs or alpha-acid units. This method helps brewers share recipes and get more consistent results among brewers. But the AAU method doesn't tell you much about what the finished beer will taste like, and it requires recalculation if you want to make a different-sized recipe.

Most brewers and beer drinkers use a system with IBUs or international bitterness units to assess and control the bitterness of beer. This measure has a direct quantitative definition that makes it an objective standard, so it's useful in a discussion of beer characteristics.

One IBU is equal to one milligram per liter of isomerized alpha acid. These isomerized or "iso" alpha acids provide bitterness in beer. They are formed when the alpha acids in hops are converted or isomerized during the boil. To determine the number of IBUs in a beer, we look at the amount of alpha acid added and estimate how much of it will be isomerized.

Fortunately, a relatively simple equation can be used for all of this:

$$\text{IBU} = (W^{oz} \times U^{\%} \times A^{\%} \times 7489)/V^{gal}$$

where W^{oz} is weight of hops in ounces; $A^\%$ is alpha acid level of hop, as a decimal (e.g., 7 percent is 0.07); $U^\%$ is percent utilization, again as a decimal (you can estimate utilization for each hop addition based on boil length, as shown below in "Basic Utilization Values"); and V^{gal} is volume of final wort in gallons.

Note: This equation is valid only for beers that have a gravity of 1.055 or less. For higher-gravity beers, a correction factor is required. This factor is $C^{gravity} = 1 + [\,(G^{boil} - 1.050)\,/\,0.2\,]$, where G^{boil} equals the specific gravity of the wort in the boil kettle. Multiply V^{gal} by this correction factor in higher-gravity beers. Use this basic formula to calculate the approximate IBU for each beer you make.

BASIC HOP UTILIZATION VALUES (U%)

BOIL TIME (minutes)	PELLET HOP UTILIZATION (percent)
Dry hop	0
0–9	8
10–19	17
20–29	21
30–44	26
45–59	29
60–74	32
75 or longer	35

70 BUILD YOUR OWN MULTITAP DISPENSER

PERHAPS BY NOW YOU'VE BECOME FANATICAL. Or you've joined or formed a club of prolific brewers. Maybe you just want a way to serve four to eight beers at one time without having to lug a million parts and pieces everywhere you go. Time to build your own multitap dispenser!

I saw several different designs for one a few years ago at the Southern California Homebrew Festival, which is held each year in Temecula, California. Each design started with a base that held the beer and kept it cool. Then taps were mounted on the top or sides of the container, so several beers could be dispensed at the same time.

The simplest model was a plastic fifty-five-gallon drum. There was room inside for four kegs, a gas bottle, and some ice, if needed. Taps were mounted around the side of the drum about ten inches apart, so beer could be served from all four taps simultaneously. The top section of the drum had been cut off about five inches below the lid to allow access to the inside. When the beer was loaded in and the connectors arranged, the top was fastened in place with those old-fashioned metal loop clasps like you used to see on trunks or footlockers. About the only drawback was that the taps were a bit low, requiring you to bend over while serving.

Another model was based on a high-tech garbage bin. It was square with two wheels and a hinged lid. A tap box was attached to the lid, and the hoses ran through a hole in the lid to the kegs below. Like the fifty-five-gallon drum model, this unit provided on-board space for kegs, coolant, and gas, as well as a self-contained area for all the connections. With the taps on top, this design is more accessible to the average beer drinker and easier to serve from. I especially like the wheels; the whole rig can be moved even when it's loaded with beer.

The granddaddy of them all was an incredible unit that held and dispensed twenty-four beers at the same time. It was based on a large insulated box that looked something like an old chest freezer. Kegs were set up in the box and connected to gas and hose fittings. The hoses ran to a serving bar on the front of the unit, where they terminated in plain old cobra-head dispensers. The cobra head sat in a hole, and in a space above each was a 3-by-5 card that described the beer. When you really need to pour a lot of beer, this is a very cool system. But I can't imagine it would be too easy to move around.

This should give you a few ideas about making a multitap system for yourself or your club. Some homebrew supply stores stock all the needed hardware. If not, just check the brewing magazines for wholesale suppliers.

Darryl Richman—Keeping It Simple

The first homebrewing Darryl Richman ever saw happened in a bathtub. "It was in Los Angeles, so they kept the fermenter in the bathtub with a bit of ice water to keep it cool," he recalls.

PROFILE

At the time, Richman thought it was an interesting home craft—a bit like making pickles or canning garden vegetables. When a friend suggested that they share the cost of buying homebrew equipment, he agreed. Richman liked the first batch, and the friend didn't, and Richman became the sole owner of the equipment.

Soon he joined the Maltose Falcons, one of the country's most active homebrewing groups, and learned all-grain brewing from other members. "I would apprentice myself out to more experienced brewers," he says. "By watching what they did and how their equipment worked, I began to understand the essentials."

One brewer always made excellent beer, but he didn't always bring beer to club meetings. When Richman went to help out with a brew, he found out why. "This guy had the most elaborate system for brewing that I've ever seen," says Richman. But the complicated equipment was always breaking down, so many batches never even made it to the fermenter. "I spent almost twenty-four hours there one weekend trying to get one batch done."

"I knew then I'd never allow myself to get carried away like that," says Richman. "I was far more interested in the finished product than the equipment."

Despite his "keep it simple" approach to equipment, Richman consistently brews outstanding beers that have won many awards. In 1990, he even took first place for *bock* beer in the National Homebrew Competition.

That netted him a trip to Norway for a week of observation at the Aass Brewery, one of the world's biggest bock producers. There he learned a great deal about commercial bock production, and he wrote a *Zymurgy* article about his experiences. Later that year, Brewers Publications asked him to write a book about bock for its Classic Beer Style Series.

"I thought a year was plenty of time to write a book," says Richman, "but with three months left, I decided I had to make another trip to Europe for more information."

Some of the German breweries wouldn't talk to him about their processes or ingredients. Others dribbled information out in small portions, testing his dedication to the project. But others offered all that they could. "One day I drove nearly 200 miles in a snowstorm to the Einbeck brewery," he recalls. "There was a pretty big language barrier, but they turned out to be very helpful."

On other trips, Richman has visited the Pilsener Urquell brewery, home of the original Pilsener-style beer. Hence, he has become closely associated with lager brewing and bock beers in particular. "I have been type cast as the 'bock guy,'" he says.

After all he's seen of brewing in other countries, Richman still finds the United States to be the most varied and open brewing community in the world. "Many breweries in Europe are very insular and provincial," he says. "Here brewers are interested in all of the different beer styles and ways of making beer. As a result, there is more information available and the whole brewing scene is more vibrant."

"That kind of diversity helps homebrewers master the language of beer and beer flavor so that they can communicate with others about beer and really enjoy the rich culture of beer that exists today."

HOLD A HONEY TASTING

MANY HOMEBREWERS HAVE used honey to make at least one beer, and these days it seems to happen more and more at the commercial level, too. When the urge strikes us, we homebrewers have also been known to knock out some mead, just for a change of pace.

Many people still view beer as a one-dimensional product, conjuring up visions of mass-produced American lager whenever the word "beer" is mentioned. Most brewers have gotten over this tendency with regard to beer, but we still tend to think of honey in much the same one-dimensional way.

In truth, though, honey is a varied substance whose character is defined by the blossoms the bees feed on. The flavor your beer gets when you brew with honey will depend in large part on the type of honey you use. Time to schedule a honey tasting!

Most large grocery stores stock three or four varietal honeys that are labeled with regard to blossom type. In natural food stores and other specialty shops, you can probably find honeys that come from six to ten different types of blossoms (see the listing of types below).

You won't need much of each kind of honey to have a tasting for your brewing buddies or homebrew club. Just a teaspoon per person of each style is plenty. You can eat the honeys straight or on a bite of bland white bread. Between samples, rinse your mouth with water (or your favorite homebrew). If you want, keep notes about the characteristics of the different types of honey, and discuss how you might use each one as an ingredient in beer or mead. If anyone has made mead from a single-blossom honey, have it available for tasting along with the source honey. Sounds like fun!

TYPES OF HONEY

Acacia—pale yellow, delicate

Alfalfa—light-colored, mild

Buckwheat—dark, full-bodied

Clover—white to amber with a pleasant mild taste

Eucalyptus—variable color, strongly flavored

Orange Blossom—light color, mild flavor, fresh scent

Heather—reddish-brown, bittersweet, aromatic

VULGARE DAY

EVERY NOW AND THEN YOU JUST HAVE to howl at the moon, and that's what Vulgare Day (pronounced vul-gar-ray) is for. Vulgare is part of the species name for barley—*Hordeum vulgare*. To me, it sounds like the perfect name for a special day when homebrewers do all the crazy things they've thought about all year, including making crazy beer.

The idea for Vulgare Day is inspired by Larry Bell at the Kalamazoo Brewing Co. Although he's a well-established commercial brewer now, Larry started out with a two-barrel system and brewed his heart out for several years until he could grow. His brewery has always had the feel of homebrew on steroids. One annual event at the brewery is Eccentric Day.

On Eccentric Day, Larry and the gang knock out a batch of strong beer. While the beer sometimes takes strange turns, the brewers are always outfitted in eccentric wear, from day-glo orange whiskers with overalls to match to Larry's favorite hand-painted tuxedo coat. After the brewing is over, they enjoy the previous year's brew at a big party. (Well, they supposedly wait until the brewing is over.)

To stage your own eccentric Vulgare Day, all you need is your brewing equipment, one to one hundred friends, and a bit of homebrew for refreshment.

For advance planning, you need focus on only one goal: making something strong. Shoot for an original gravity of at least 1.080, so the beer will age gracefully. After that, anything goes. Pull open the cabinet and see what leaps out at you. If it's edible (and doesn't contain much fat or protein), you can put it in your beer. Ginger, vanilla beans, and star anise are obvious choices; Ceylon tea, tree ears, and mangoes are a bit less obvious. A pinch of snuff, a pop of Scotch, and a slice of habañero will definitely spice things up.

Just remember one thing: next year, you must drink this beer. You're not allowed to throw it out.

If people in your group are the cautious types who question whether those little pickled corns will complement the overall flavor of your creation, just ignore them. But instead of adding the whole jar, just throw in one or two for effect.

One bit of convention you won't want to cast aside is record-keeping. Although it's unlikely you would ever want to reproduce exactly the same beer, brewing notes that list everything added (and by whom) will make entertaining reading when you're tasting this a year from now.

Plan your own Vulgare Day sometime in the next 113 days.

WORLD'S LONGEST BEER RUN

YOU HAVE A PARTY. EVERYBODY chips in ten bucks for beer and twenty bucks to help pay for the trip to get beer for the next party. At the end of the night, you have a drawing—and somebody wins a ticket to a beer capital of Europe, leaving the next day.

This is just a beery variation on the old suitcase party. Come to the party with your suitcase packed, because someone will win a round-trip ticket to Europe. (Or, say, Portland, Oregon, if your budget is tight.) The trip should commence within twenty-four hours, and the traveler has but one responsibility: bring back good beer for the next gathering of the clan. You might even supply the traveler with a list of things to get and a luggage cart to carry it all. Oh—and don't forget to give them some cash for the beer.

Everyone who bought a chance gets to enjoy the beer the winner brings back. Just plan another party for a week or two later.

Sounds like a good annual event.

74 THIS BEER WILL COOK YOUR GOOSE

A BREWER WHO WORKED AT A LARGE regional brewery tells the story of the annual bad batch of beer. For several years, there was always one really bad batch that finished fermentation in early January. He discovered the cause when he walked into the brewhouse during the third shift one night before Christmas to find several ropes tied to the outside of the brew kettle and disappearing into the bubbling brew. It turns out the workers were in the habit of cooking their Christmas turkeys in the boiling wort. The results were great for Christmas dinner, but they didn't do much for the beer!

I've tried this with chicken, and the results are great. You could expand it next time you cook a turkey, or scale it down for a chicken or smaller fowl like a Rock Cornish game hen.

WORT-CRUSTED CHICKEN
In a 2-gallon or larger pot, combine:
1 gallon water
1.5–2.5 pounds malt extract (type and color are your choice)
Bring this to a boil, and then add:
3 pounds chicken pieces (with bones and skin)
Optional: add four to six hop pellets 15 minutes into the boil

Boil for 30 minutes. Near the end of the boil, preheat the oven to 450 °F (232 °C). Remove the chicken from the wort and place it in a baking dish or pan. Bake 15 to 20 minutes.

When you're done, discard the leftover wort—or you can try your hand at Idea 41: Cock Ale.

SEND YOUR BEER ON A CRUISE

INDIA PALE ALE WAS CREATED for shipment from England to India, where it was consumed by thirsty British imperialists. The beer was brewed to an original gravity of 1.065–1.070, and it was well attenuated, reaching terminal gravities as low as 1.012 even before it left the brewery. This low residual gravity, along with a very high hop rate, was designed to help protect the beer from "fetters," or infections, during its long voyage.

Those who have sought to recreate the flavor of the original India pale ale have often looked for a way to simulate the passage to India. The trip not only aged the beer, but also exposed it to constant agitation from the movement of the boat on the waves. These combined influences almost certainly had a strong influence on its flavor and character.

James McCrorie of the Craft Brewing Association in England is one who has researched and brewed in pursuit of the perfect India pale ale. One innovation he came up with was to send his beer to sea for the summer. After brewing a batch, he put it in a soda keg (bottles would work, too) and stowed it in his boat. Hidden from the sun and cooled by the nearby water, this type of strong ale should keep well for three to six months. When the summer ends, the resulting beer should have experienced enough "action" to qualify as a reasonable simulation of its world-traveling kin. Here's my recipe:

A NICE INDIA PALE ALE (makes 5 gallons)
Target original gravity: 1.065
Start with 12 pounds of English pale ale malt and mash at 149 °F (65 °C) for 45 to 60 minutes. Alternately, mini-mash 3 pounds of pale ale malt at 150 °F (65 °C)

and combine this with 5.5 pounds of dry pale malt extract or two cans (6.6 pounds) of pale malt extract syrup.

For hops, use proper East Kent Goldings or the American variety, Willamettes. For a more innovative brew, acquire some of the English Challenger hops. Use 12 to 13 alpha-acid units of bittering hops, boiled for 75 to 90 minutes. Make additions of flavor and aroma hops as follows: 0.75 ounce boiled 20 minutes, 0.75 ounce boiled 2 minutes, and 0.5 ounce dry-hopped in secondary or a soda keg. Use a good attenuating yeast, preferably English.

76

HERE'S A COOL FERMENTATION IDEA

ENGLISH BREWERS OFTEN USE ATTEMPERATION coils inside the fermenters to help control the temperature of fermentation. In one sense, these attemperation coils are the same as a standard homebrewer's immersion wort chiller: copper coils with cold water running through them to carry off excess heat. In fact, I've seen an English homebrew setup with a wort chiller placed in an open fermenter. The wort chiller was fed with cold water that was recirculated by a small pump. With just a little effort, any homebrewer could create a similar—or improved—arrangement. The whole thing requires three elements:

(1)   Fermenter with cooling coil wrapped around it or inserted inside
(2)   Bucket filled with ice and water, outlet at bottom, return at top
(3)   Pump to pump the water around, plugged into a temperature-control switch from your local homebrew shop

You can imagine various arrangements for the fermenter and cooling coil setup. You could wrap copper tubing around a glass fermenter or soda keg, and then insulate the whole arrangement by wrapping it in bubble pack. Alternately, you could use a plastic fermenter and drop your wort chiller right in the middle.

Just about any bucket will do for the water-and-ice reservoir. If it has an outlet at the bottom with a hose barb, so much the better. An insulated mash/lauter tun would probably be ideal. (For details on building a simple one, see Idea 6: Longing to Lauter.) If you have a dedicated beer 'fridge, you might rig a way to keep this cold-water reservoir inside, thereby reducing the need for regular additions of fresh ice.

For most homebrewers, the toughest part of this arrangement is the pump. If you're really nuts about brewing, you could invest in a small centrifugal food-grade pump you can use for beer. But for this project, a small utility or immersible pump from your hardware store should do. Just plug it into one of those refrigerator temperature controllers for sale at most homebrew stores. Put the temperature probe in the beer, and dial in the temperature you want. The pump will cycle on whenever the beer gets too warm, and the needed cooling will be provided.

This device can be used to cool ale fermentations during the summer or in extremely warm brewing areas. You might also be able to use it to achieve lager fermentation temps under some circumstances.

Tim and Dot Artz—Still Brewin' after All These Years

Since 1985, the making of fermented beverages has been a major pastime for Tim and Dot Artz. Along the way, they've made just about every style of beer and a variety of other related beverages such as mead and cider. Given this long and varied history, it's not surprising that they are leading members of the BURP (Brewers United for Real Potables) homebrew club in Washington, D.C.

PROFILE

Like many long-time homebrewers, the Artzes found beer by way of wine. Tim used to order grapes in bulk, picking them up at the harbor in Baltimore. Production started with the help of friends who provided a classic foot-stomping for the grapes before they were put through a press. "We actually made some pretty good wine at one point," says Dot.

This early interest in wine may be reflected in the couple's continuing interest in making fruit meads. "We always have a lot of fruit around," says Tim. "We've used it to make quite a variety of meads over the years, so right now we have a really nice stockpile of meads that are in prime condition."

But the interest in fruit didn't end with wine and mead. One year Tim had "a truck full" of pears. Some of it went into making mead, but a good bit became "peary," or cider made from pears. "That year I spent nearly twelve hours crushing pears and wound up with ten or twelve gallons of pear juice to ferment," says Tim.

Another area of brewing that the couple explored was the production of Belgian beers. In 1994, Tim organized an event called the Spirit of Belgium—a weekend-long study of Belgian beers and brewing techniques that included speakers, tastings, and a homebrew competition. As this was being organized, Dot got the bug to do a *lambic.*

"I put together a partial mash-and-extract recipe for lambic that included raw wheat," she says. When the brewing was done, Tim took over management of the fermentation, employing the collection of yeasts and bacteria that commonly affect lambics. After several months, they added cherries they had picked. "That beer took second best of show at the Spirit of Free Beer competition in 1995," recalls Dot.

By now, Tim and Dot have produced several hundred batches of beer, mead, and cider. Along the way, they have put a lot of time and energy into the hobby. For instance, Tim has organized bulk grain purchases for club members. "He pulled into our driveway with two tons of malt in fifty-pound bags," recalls Dot. "The two of us carried all of it down into our basement."

Then there was the day Tim called in sick at work so he could stay home to brew. Unfortunately, it turned out to be the coldest day of the year, and all of his brewing equipment is designed for outdoor use. Undaunted, he brewed on. Still, he had a lot of explaining to do the next day when he went to work with red, wind-burned cheeks.

Where do they get all their recipes? Tim says they come from his head. "I don't think I've ever brewed someone else's recipe," he says. "I just think about what flavors I want in the finished beer and then I put in what is needed to achieve that."

Anyone who wants to learn this skill can do it the same way Tim and Dot did: watching more experienced brewers, talking to them, and, most importantly, sampling their beers.

77

FORGET ABOUT YOUR BEER TO IMPROVE ITS FLAVOR

ENGLISH BREWERS HAVE LONG PRODUCED a type of beer called "old ale." It is aged before distribution, which allows development of flavors that wouldn't be found in the fresh product. Consumers once found this aging so desirable that early porters and stouts routinely included a portion of well-aged product.

Today, freshness of beer is emphasized, simply because today's average beer gets worse with age, not better. Still, among the strong English beers, we continue to find brewery-aged products. Examples include Thomas Hardy's Ale, Gale's Prize Old Ale, and Green King's 5X. In addition, American, Belgian, and German producers of strong beers will tell you their products often improve with age.

Any beer with a starting gravity above about 1.065 is a candidate for aging. And the higher the gravity, the longer the beer is likely to mature and improve. The makers of Thomas Hardy's Ale (original gravity: 1.120) suggest it will improve and keep for up to twenty-five years. A strong homebrewed beer I made four years ago continues to mature and improve.

As a homebrewer, one of the joys to experience is the gradual maturation of your product over the years. If you put away a whole case, you can sample a bottle every six months or so to note the subtle flavor changes and the softening and mixing of the initial sharp characteristics. Your patience will be rewarded, and—if you save enough to share with others—you'll find your stature and reputation as a brewer improves.

To store your beer for many years, you'll need a suitable location: someplace cool that is protected from light. I keep my choicest stock in a cool area under a sink, but basements, closets, and even some storage areas will do. Keep the beer from freezing, keep it from getting any warmer than 70 °F (21 °C), if possible, and protect it from light. After that, forget about it!

A SOFT SPOT FOR PRETZELS

I'VE TALKED ELSEWHERE ABOUT *BREZEN,* the German-style soft pretzels some-times eaten with *weizen* beer. In most communities, a good hard pretzel is rare, and good soft ones are nearly impossible to find. But it's not hard to make your own. And don't worry if you're fresh out of weizen; brezen go great with any kind of beer!

SOFT PRETZELS
1 tablespoon or 1 package active dry yeast
2.5–3 cups all-purpose flour
2 tablespoons vegetable oil
1 tablespoon malt extract syrup
6 tablespoons baking soda
1 tablespoon coarse salt

Put 1 cup of warm water in a mixing bowl, and dissolve the yeast in it. Add the malt extract, the oil, and 1.5 cups of the flour. Mix for several minutes until smooth. Stir in additional flour until a soft dough has formed. Spread flour on a clean, flat surface where you can knead the dough. Knead for about 5 minutes, adding flour as needed whenever the dough is sticky. After kneading, form the dough into a ball and place it in a greased bowl in a warm place. Allow the dough to rise for about an hour or until it has doubled in size.

On the floured surface, punch the dough and split it into a dozen pieces of approximately equal size. Roll each piece into a rope about 18 inches long and the diameter of a pencil. Then twist into pretzel shape. (At this point, the pretzels should be kind of skinny and anemic. Remember they'll puff up a good bit before they're done.) Fill a greased cookie sheet with these pretzels, put the cookie sheet in a warm place, and allow the pretzels to rise until puffy. While they're rising, add the baking soda to 6 cups of water and bring the mixture to a boil.

Preheat your oven to 425 °F (218 °C). When the pretzels are puffy, use a slotted spoon to boil each pretzel individually for 10 seconds on each side. After boiling, hold the pretzel in the spoon and let the water drain back into the pot. Put the pretzel back on the cookie sheet. After all the pretzels have been boiled and returned to the cookie sheet, sprinkle coarse salt over them. Pop the tray into the oven and bake 15 to 20 minutes until the pretzels are brown.

When finished, enjoy with your favorite beer. Mustard is optional.

79

BIG BAD BARLEY WINE

THESE DAYS, ONLY A FEW commercial brewers in the United States and the United Kingdom produce the type of really strong ale once commonplace in England. During the mid-1800s, English brewers designated their beers using a series of "X" marks. At the high end, the XXX and XXXX beers routinely had gravities of 1.100, and some reached as high as 1.140!

Because such strong beers are rare today, you'll have to make your own if you want to enjoy the complex character and flavor they can deliver. I chose the occasion of my one-hundredth batch of homebrew to crank out the beer whose recipe is shown in this activity. The goal was to produce a beer with 1.100 OG and 100 international bitterness units. Be forewarned: this type of beer will not be ready to drink in two weeks, or even two months. Give it a good two years before it really starts to come into peak condition.

BATCH 100 BARLEY WINE
Malts
10 pounds pale ale malt
4.5 pounds light, dry malt extract
3 pounds wheat malt
3 pounds biscuit malt, home-toasted amber malt, etc.
3 pounds Crystal malt of various types (mix colors, maltsters)

Mash grains at 150 °F (65 °C). Add extract in boil.

Hops

30 alpha-acid units bittering hops, boiled for 60 minutes
1.5 ounces Cascade hops, add 15 minutes before end of boil
1 ounce Northern Brewer hops, add 5 minutes before end of boil
0.5 ounce Cascade hops, add 5 minutes before end of boil

Aerate aggressively before fermentation. Pitch with a large starter (I used 3 quarts) or 1 cup of thick yeast slurry. Allow a long secondary fermentation (four to six weeks), and then bottle it and forget about it for at least two years.

80

MAKE YOUR OWN CASK ALE

THE REAL ALE MOVEMENT, active in the United Kingdom for more than twenty-five years, is now growing in U.S. interest. Real ale is never filtered or artificially carbonated. The Campaign for Real Ale defines it as "a name for a draft (or bottled) beer brewed from traditional ingredients, matured by secondary fermentation in the container from which it is dispensed, and served without the use of extraneous carbon dioxide." Nearly all bottled homebrew is real ale according to this definition!

But the true focus of real ale is cask ale. These days, most casks are stainless steel rather than wood, but they still offer a unique and interesting dispensing method. As with beer kegs of old, you must hammer a tap through a wood-plugged hole in the front of the cask to serve the beer. (Little wooden spiles are inserted in the bung to relieve excess pressure before the keg is tapped.) Finally, isinglass and carrageen finings are used to help clarify the beer so it is "star bright" when consumed.

The casks found in the United States are called firkins. They hold nine imperial gallons, or something just short of eleven U.S. gallons. At this volume, it's just within reach of the homebrewer to produce enough beer to fill a firkin—and some enterprising souls have started to do so.

You can procure a new firkin, tap, and the needed supplies for somewhere around $150. Then brew eleven gallons of beer, ferment it, and rack it into the firkin.

With a little research, you can master the art of fining in the cask so the beer will be completely clear when you serve it—but for family and friends, a bit of haze won't hurt. Also, remember all the yeast and haze settle to the bottom—so set the cask in one place after you fill it, and leave it there until it's empty!

In a week or two, when the beer is ready to drink, have a party. The beer in the cask is exposed to the air when it's dispensed, so it won't be good for more than a few days once you draw the first pint. Invite some thirsty friends over, and enjoy.

HOLD A HOMEBREW EXPO

NO MATTER HOW MANY HOMEBREWERS you know in your area, there are probably a bunch more you haven't met. Then there are all those folks who want to homebrew, but haven't gotten around to trying it yet.

A fun way to bring these folks together is to stage a homebrew expo. And, although the basic idea is similar to a trade show, you don't need to rent the local convention center.

For several years, the Chicago Beer Society held homebrew expos twice a year in the events room at our local brewpub. Friendly bars and restaurants near you may be an option. All you really need is a room where you can set up some exhibit tables and let people wander around. In addition, serve some light food and, of course, beer—both homebrewed and otherwise.

As for exhibitors, contact all of the local homebrew shops, brewpubs, microbreweries, and beer bars. Invite them to set up exhibits and encourage them to promote the expo by distributing flyers or exhibiting posters. Rather than charging them for the table, you could just ask them to donate raffle items. Other possible exhibitors from your area include other homebrew clubs, locally distributed beer periodicals, and homebrew equipment makers or suppliers.

It's easier to attract exhibitors if you have a promotion plan. Homebrew club newsletters are one way to reach potential attendees. In Chicago, we also usually do a mailing to all American Homebrewers Association members within a one-hundred-mile radius. In addition, you can send a press release to local newspapers, announce the expo at other beer festivals, and put an ad in a local paper.

Activities can help to attract people. The most obvious would be demonstrations that show people how to homebrew. Or give talks on special brewing topics like mashing, fruit beers, or British beer. At some point during the event, hold a raffle and give away items donated by the shops and suppliers.

Finally, use some of the ideas in this book: serve beer foods, have a judges' corner, try to stump the experts, or do a malted barley tasting.

To make these events work economically, we've always held them at an "off" time—for instance, Thursday evening or Sunday afternoon. This makes it easier to reserve the facility and to arrange workable pricing. If you charge a modest admission price, the expo is usually affordable for the attendees and the club.

82

SPEED YOUR GRAIN DRAIN

IF YOU'VE STARTED MASHING GRAINS, you know the touchiest part of the whole process is lautering, when you let the wort run off of the grains. Lautering can be very slow—especially if you use grains other than barley in your brew. Wheat, oats, and rye all get used in beer from time to time. Although it's possible to lauter mashes that contain small quantities of these grains, you'll need a little help with larger quantities. For instance, you might decide to make a wheat wine—it has the strength of barley wine, but it's made mostly from malted wheat rather than malted barley. Another example is rye *weizen*, which substitutes rye for wheat.

The secret to lautering these gummy mashes is rice hulls. They are thin and hard, almost like little shards of glass. Mixed into a mash, they dramatically improve the flow of fluid through the grain bed.

Some homebrew stores stock rice hulls. To use them, simply rinse the hulls in clean water using a strainer or grain bag, and then stir them into your mash. Just a few cups will be sufficient for a ten-pound mash.

Even if you don't plan to do a special-grain brew any time soon, keep a small supply of rice hulls on hand. You can never tell when you'll have a sticky mash that could use some help.

TRAVEL THROUGH TIME WITH BEER

WHETHER YOU'RE JUST STARTING out or you're looking for a way to commemorate twenty years of brewing, a homebrew time capsule can provide lots of fun.

Pick a container, fill it with homebrew and related stuff, and seal it up for a long rest. A five-year wait will be interesting, ten years even more so. And if you are really looking for some future fun, pack your beery time capsule away for twenty or twenty-five years.

What should go in the time capsule? Beer, for starters. I'd go for strong, bottle-conditioned beers like barley wine and imperial stout. Mead would be good, too. Then throw in a commemorative glass from the latest beer festival, a copy of your favorite beer magazine or recipe, and photos of your latest homebrew get-together. Be sure to include notes about the items in case your memory fades in the intervening years.

SMOKIN' GOOD CHILI

IF YOU LOVE GOOD CHILI, YOU OUGHT to try spicing up your next batch with some smoked malt.

   Here's the plan: buy or make some smoked malt. Mash a pound or so, and collect the wort. By using this wort as the base for your chili, you'll get some nice smoked flavor as well as malt character. Mmmm!

SPICE AND EASY

FELLOW CHICAGO BEER SOCIETY MEMBER Randy Mosher has devised a great way to control the addition of spices to beer. Rather than adding the spices directly, he uses potions instead.

To make a potion, spike cheap vodka with various herbs and spices. Once the potion is complete, you can add a small amount to one glass of beer to figure out the dosage you'll need. From there, it's just a matter of multiplication to determine the amount to use in the whole batch.

To make your potion, put the spices you want to experiment with in a jar, or put individual spices in their own jars. Next, add vodka to each jar. Cover the spices completely, and make sure the total volume of vodka is at least twice that of the spice. Virtually any spice can be used in a potion—one Mosher potion mixed black pepper, coriander, vanilla, and star anise. What you add is up to you.

The potion will be ready to use in a week or two. At that point, get out your measuring cup and spoons. Draw yourself eight ounces of beer, add half a teaspoon of potion, and taste. If the spice flavor isn't strong enough, add more potion. If it's too strong, start over with a fresh eight-ounce glass of beer and add one-quarter teaspoon of potion on the next try. When you have a mixture you like, determine how much potion to add for a whole five-gallon batch. These guidelines should help.

1/4 teaspoon in 8 ounces = 4 teaspoons in 5 gallons
1/2 teaspoon in 8 ounces = 8 teaspoons in 5 gallons
3/4 teaspoon in 8 ounces = 12 teaspoons (4 tablespoons) in 5 gallons
1 teaspoon in 8 ounces = 16 teaspoons (5 tablespoons plus 1 teaspoon) in 5 gallons

SMOKED PORTER CHEESECAKE

FOR YEARS, THE FOLKS at Alaskan Brewing Company have made an award-winning smoked porter. Their product captures the spirit of homebrewing. Cold-smoked over Alaskan alder wood, the grain takes three days to prepare. The resulting beer is a unique seasonal specialty that is much sought after in Alaska and the Pacific Northwest.

Although there's never enough smoked porter to fill all the orders, the brewery still promotes the beer with tasty recipe suggestions. This one is a nice addition to any homebrewer's recipe book.

Only a lucky few will be able to snag bottles of Alaskan Smoked Porter for this recipe. The rest of us can certainly make up a nice smoked porter of our own. (See Idea 23: Barbecue Your Malt for That Tangy, Smoked Beer Flavor.) Alternately, you might try this with another complex malty beer like a *bock* or imperial stout.

SMOKED PORTER CHEESECAKE
24 ounces cream cheese at room temperature
3/4 cup granulated sugar
3/4 cup light brown sugar
1 1/2 teaspoons salt
1 tablespoon vanilla
6 eggs at room temperature
2 pints sour cream at room temperature
1/3 cup cornstarch
24 ounces smoked porter beer
1 cup cookie crumbs (shortbread)

Heat oven to 350 °F (177 °C). Boil beer until it's reduced to 3/4 cup. Set aside to cool.

Combine cream cheese and sugars and mix until blended. Add salt, vanilla, and eggs (one at a time), beating until mixture is smooth. Add sour cream, cornstarch, and 3/4 cup reduced beer, and blend.

Press cookie crumbs into the bottom of a lightly greased springform (or equivalent) pan. Carefully pour batter into the bottom of the pan and smooth until level. Place in oven with a pan of water on the rack beneath, and bake 1 hour and 45 minutes or until center is set but still jiggles. Remove and cool overnight in the refrigerator. Serve chilled with fresh raspberries and glasses of smoked porter.

Lion, Tigers, and Bugs! A few years ago, a homebrewer named Ralph bought his first fifty-pound bag of malt. He brought it home on a Friday and tossed it on the floor in his basement before going away for the weekend.

When Ralph next looked at his bag of malt, on Monday evening, one corner was missing and a trail of grain led from the bag to the nearby laundry area. A little checking turned up a hole in the wall behind the dryer, through which rodents had come in to pillage.

BLOOPERS

Not long after that incident, Ralph ordered five pounds of imported specialty malt from an out-of-state supplier. It arrived packaged in a crisp new brown paper bag. Ralph put the new acquisition in the cabinet with his other malt supplies.

When he finally got around to using the specialty malt a few weeks later, he noticed something odd. Many of the kernels had a perfectly round little hole in the side. Fearing the worst, Ralph dumped the whole bag out into a bowl. What he found was a host of tiny black bugs—grain mites, he was later told.

Ralph threw out the malt and its bag, but his problems weren't over. Weeks later he opened a different bag of malt and found more of the same bugs. This bag was plastic, but the top was gathered and closed with a twist-tie fastener, and the tiny mites had found their way in.

Eventually, Ralph threw out a good deal of malt and thoroughly cleaned the cabinet. Now he uses nothing but zip-lock bags for malt storage, and he hasn't had any more problems with grain mites.

Every brewer knows that unfermented beer is the ideal food for most microorganisms. It's rich in sugar, protein, and other nutrients. We spend a good deal of time making sure that what grows in wort is the specific strain of yeast we selected for the job—not some other organism.

With all the effort we expend to keep from feeding unwanted beasties in the fermenter, we sometimes forget to safeguard our supplies. Malt is a wonderful food source—and a wide variety of visible bugs and four-legged creatures will do their best to get at it.

911 FOR BREWERS

YOU CAN DO THIS AS A CLUB ACTIVITY or as a service to homebrewers in your area. The idea is to give homebrewers someone they can call whenever they need help with a brewing question.

Organization is easy. Find four or five local homebrewers who really know their stuff. Enlist their support to answer questions periodically—say one weekend each month. Then simply publish a schedule of on-call brewers and their phone numbers.

If you really want to go all out, get the local pager company to donate one of its units. Then whoever is on call can carry the pager and respond to the urgent calls from distressed homebrewers.

This kind of system will help your club bring in new members, and it also gives current members the support they need to tackle new brewing challenges.

TASTING TREATS

SOONER OR LATER, YOU'LL have some homebrew you want to show off to your friends at a beer tasting. To add appeal to the event, include a wide range of beer styles—from basic Pilsener to oatmeal stout—and some high-quality snacks.

Cheese is always popular. It goes well with beer, and the selection is broad at many stores these days. Start with a good sharp cheddar and a well-aged brie. Throw in smoked gouda, some Stilton, and a sample of goat cheese, and you'll have a nice range of flavors to complement nearly any beer.

Bread is another popular tasting food. Nearly any bakery offers sourdough, multigrain, and dark loaves. Some even make specialty breads using whole grains, nuts, vegetables, or spices. For another interesting twist, use bagels or add spreads to the mix.

For a more light-hearted tasting, make up your own smorgasbord of pop-culture foods. Themes might include fried foods (okra, cheese, and shrimp could round out a menu that begins with French fries and onion rings), pizza products (both frozen and fresh), ball-park fare or an ethnic mishmash (Indian papadams, Chinese moo-shu, Italian ziti, and Greek gyros.) You could assemble it all yourself or assign each guest one food item and one beer style. During the tasting, mix and match the foods with the beers until you find the perfect pairings.

FILL YOUR TANKARD WITH LAMBSWOOL

ON THE FIRST OF NOVEMBER, the English used to pay homage to the angel of fruits and berries. This day came to be known as Lambswool—although this word probably evolved from an earlier name that meant "the day of apples." Appropriately enough, a warm, apple-based beverage consumed on that day was known as lambswool. Use a bottle or two of a malty homebrewed ale to mix up your own lambswool.

LAMBSWOOL (for an 8-ounce mug)
4 ounces malty strong ale
4 ounces apple juice (fresh-squeezed or organic, if possible)
2 teaspoons brown sugar
1 small pinch nutmeg
1 small pinch grated ginger root

If you like this, make a portion for the kids by substituting milk for the ale!

90

BAPPIR BREW

THE OLDEST RECIPE KNOWN is an ancient Sumerian hymn that describes the making of beer. Inhabitants of both Mesopotamia and Egypt made beer from bread, the Egyptian version of which was known as *bappir.* The beverages were widely enjoyed in both cultures, leading some academics to speculate that beer, not bread, caused nomads to settle into a fixed-site agrarian lifestyle.

In the early 1990s, Fritz Maytag of Anchor Brewing collaborated with university scholar Solomon Katz to research and brew a similar beer called Ninkasi. The articles they wrote don't provide a real recipe, but Maytag and Katz's brew started with bread made from honey and flour with both malted and unmalted barley. It was baked twice and had a texture reminiscent of biscotti with granola in it. In the mash, this bappir was mixed with twice its weight in malt plus a generous measure of dates. Aged samples of the resulting brew were said to have a champagnelike effervescence, a flavor like hard apple cider, and a subtle but detectable aroma of dates.

If you want to feel a kinship with the ancient brewers of bappir beer, toss a loaf of whole-grain bread into your next mash. (Be sure to get a loaf with no preservatives!) Or, for a more ambitious alternative, try whipping up a couple gallons of your own bappir beer following this recipe. Extract brewers, don't worry about the use of grain—this recipe requires no mashing equipment.

Bappir brew is made in three stages: bread making, cooking, and fermentation. First, make the bread.

BAPPIR BREAD
1 pound two-row Pilsener or pale ale malt
1 2/3 cups barley flour

1 2/3 cups whole-wheat flour
1/2 cup honey
2 cups warm water

Put the crushed grain in a large bowl and add the honey and water. Stir until the grain is evenly wet. Add the flour in three additions of approximately 1 cup each. After each addition, mix the dough until it is free of dry areas and lumps. (After the second addition of flour, you'll probably want to start using your hands to do the mixing.) When all the flour has been mixed in, the dough will be slightly sticky. Make it into a ball; then squash it down so you have a round loaf about 1 1/4 to 1 1/2 inches thick and 8 to 10 inches across. Let it sit for an hour and then bake on a nonstick baking sheet in a 350-°F (177-°C) oven for 90 minutes. At the end of the 90 minutes, turn off the oven, but leave the loaf inside until the oven is cool.

Now you're ready to use the bappir bread in making bappir beer.

BAPPIR BEER
1 pound whole dates with no preservatives
1 package dry ale yeast

You'll need a plastic bucket-type fermenter or other wide-mouth container to ferment bappir beer. When I made this, I used my brewing pot and left the mixture of dates and grain in the covered pot through the first three days of fermentation. In any case, before you begin making the beer, decide on a fermenter, and then clean and sanitize it.

Put 2.5 gallons of cold water in a pot and add the dates. Heat, stirring occasionally. When it comes to a boil, turn off the heat and let it sit 15 minutes. During this time, you may want to recite the ancient hymn to Ninkasi in the ancient Sumerian tongue, just for good luck.

Now break the bappir bread into small pieces and add the pieces to the mixture of hot water and dates. Stir well, and then use two large spoons to break up the pieces of bread and crush the dates. At this point in the process, the brew bears a strong resemblance to chicken soup. But don't worry; the Pharaohs will love it.

After about 10 minutes of mixing, add 1 pound of crushed two-row malt. Stir well and then let settle. Allow this mixture to cool to room temperature; usually overnight will do the trick. Or, after the first few hours, you can put it in the refrigerator to speed cooling. Next, pour the mixture into the fermenter and pitch the yeast.

After two to three days of fermentation, siphon the liquid from the grains and dates. Sanitize a strainer and press it into the fermenting muck to create a pool of liquid you can siphon off into a regular fermenter.

When I did this, I wound up with about 2 gallons of beer in secondary fermentation. After a week or so, prime and bottle. When carbonated, this beer is a slightly tart, citruslike beverage with the distinct taste of dates.

91

CELEBRATE A WEDDING WITH BRIDE ALE

ENGLISHMEN (AND WOMEN!) USED TO CELEBRATE matrimony in much the same way we do today, but with an exception. Bickerdyke's *Curiosities of Ale and Beer* tells us that in the 1500s, it was a common custom for the bride to "sell" ale on the wedding day. This selling was a bit unorthodox, in that wedding guests were expected to pay, according to their ability, with money or a gift. The proceeds were intended to help the new couple establish their household. Today, guests bring gifts to a wedding reception—but too often these days, the ale is missing.

As a brewer, you can help to preserve the roots of this tradition by brewing up a bride ale when you or someone you know ties the knot. The beer can be a welcome addition to the bachelor party, the rehearsal dinner, or the wedding reception itself. Just be sure to check it out with the bride beforehand!

If you have a lick of artistic talent, or graphic resources at your disposal, labels add a custom touch to this type of project. (Consider using twenty-two-ounce bottles. In addition to reducing the bottling chores, they're easy for people to share and they give you more room for label design.)

For general consumption, you'll want a bride ale that is lighter-colored and less bitter than many other homebrews. Still, it can be tasty, with plenty of hop flavor and aroma to balance the malt. The beer I've designed for this purpose packs a little extra punch for celebration purposes, and it relies on European-type hops to provide an attractive floral, perfumy aroma.

At some weddings, separate beers may be served for the bride and the groom. If you want to make a bride's version out of this recipe, add fruit flavoring of your choice to half the batch after secondary fermentation.

JUNE-BUG BRIDE ALE (makes 5 gallons)

Expected original gravity: 1.055–1.060

3 pounds two-row or Pilsener malt

4 pounds Alexander's Sun Country light malt extract syrup

1.5 pounds ultralight or light dry malt extract

3 alpha-acid units bittering hops (select from varieties listed in the following ingredient)

1 ounce Saaz, Hallertau, Tettnang, Spalt, Liberty, Crystal, or Mt. Hood added in two additions—half an ounce 20 minutes before the end of the boil and the other half 2 minutes before the end of the boil

Mini-mash the crushed grains, or soak them in water at about 150 °F (65 °C) for an hour. Remove grains with a strainer or grain bag. Add the extracts and bittering hops to the resulting wort, and bring to a boil. After boiling 40 minutes, add 1/2 ounce of flavor hops. After boiling 18 additional minutes, add 1/2 ounce of aroma hops. Two minutes later, turn off the heat and begin your usual wort-chilling procedure.

SPRUCE UP YOUR BEER

LIKE SMOKED GERMAN *RAUCHBIER* or tart Belgian lambics, spruce-flavored beers are a rare specialty. Those who have fallen in love with them admit it might take a pint or two to acquire a taste for these piney potions. But many who try them become converts for life.

Spruce extracts are available through most homebrew supply shops, but if you live where black or red spruce trees can be found, you can collect your own fresh spruce tips to experiment with.

Black spruce *(Picea mariana)* is also known as bog spruce, swamp spruce, or shortleaf black spruce. It grows in most of Canada and Alaska and is commonly found in the northern United States as far south as central Minnesota, Rhode Island, and Massachusetts. Occasionally it grows as far south as southern Wisconsin, southern Michigan, Pennsylvania, and New Jersey.

Red spruce *(Picea rubens)* is also known as yellow spruce, West Virginia spruce, eastern spruce, he-balsam, and blue spruce. It's found in Canada and farther south in the United States, reaching to eastern West Virginia, northern and western Virginia, western North Carolina, and eastern Tennessee.

The springtime shoots or tips from these trees are ideal for flavoring beer. They can be added directly during the boil or saved for year-round use as an extract. To make the extract, cover a large handful of shoots with water and boil until the water is strongly flavored.

Dark beers seem to go best with spruce flavor. To make a dark spruce beer, boil shoots or extract for an hour, much as you would with hops. Here's a basic recipe for exploring spruce beer.

NOW HERE'S THE PITCH (makes 5 gallons)

6.6 pounds pale or light malt extract (2 cans extract syrup), or use 6 pounds dry
    malt extract

1 pound dark Crystal malt, crushed

0.5 pound chocolate malt, crushed

0.25 pound roast barley, crushed

5–6 alpha-acid units Cascade or Centennial hops

1 ounce spruce essence, or use 1 large handful of spruce tips (remove with hops)

Ale yeast

Combine the crushed grains in a large grain bag. Put them in 2 gallons of cold water in a pot on the stove. Turn on the heat. Stir the grain bag every few minutes. When the water starts to boil, turn off the heat and remove the grains, leaving behind as much liquid from them as possible. Now add the malt extract, hops, and spruce essence. Turn on the heat, bring to a boil, and boil 60 minutes. Let stand for 5 minutes, and then chill. Transfer to the fermenter and pitch with your favorite ale yeast.

VANILLA MALT FREEZE

EVEN THE MOST BEER-O-PHOBIC member of your family will go for this tasty treat. It's ice cream made with malt extract and just a touch of vanilla—great with chocolate sauce and a nice dry stout.

If you don't have an ice-cream maker, beg, borrow, or steal one. Or substitute vanilla ice cream for the half-and-half, and mix the whole thing up in the blender.

VANILLA MALT FREEZE (makes 2 quarts)
2 eggs
1/2 cup sugar
1 cup milk
2 cups half-and-half
3/4 cup malt pale extract (dry or syrup)
1/2 teaspoon vanilla extract

Whip the two eggs in a mixing bowl that's large enough to hold all the ingredients. Mix in the sugar a little at a time, and whip the mixture for 2 to 3 minutes. Finally, add the remaining ingredients and blend. If you use dry extract, you'll have to be pretty aggressive to get all the lumps out.

Freeze in the ice-cream maker and enjoy!

PLAN A BREWER'S TOUR OF EUROPE

THE CULTURE OF BEER EMANATES from Europe, so there's much for a brewer to see and do on the other side of the Atlantic. If you go in winter, you'll find activity at every brewery—and brewers who are often happy to chat for a few minutes about their craft. Best of all, air fares are less expensive that time of year.

If you do some research, you can arrange to stay at inns associated with breweries or pubs in nearly every area. They're usually clean and reasonably priced, and they're close to the important attractions in each city—namely the beer! As for getting from place to place, the trains are okay, but if there are several people, renting a car is just as economical and quite a bit faster.

Fax the brewery ahead of time to inquire about tours. Some breweries make special attempts to accommodate American homebrewers, whereas others want you to join a regularly scheduled public tour. Also ask if the brewery offers overnight accommodations and, if not, what they recommend in the area.

Whatever you do, don't schedule too many activities for yourself. You'll want plenty of time to sit and enjoy the local beers and culture. In many pubs, the locals speak English, and they're fascinated to learn that you've come all this way just to drink their beer.

As for cities to visit—everyone knows Munich is famous for beer. A stop there is definitely worthwhile. If you get there, don't miss the nearby Hallertau hop region, where you can eat, drink, and spend the night at the Auer Brewery (Au in der Hallertau). Other stops I highly recommend are Bamburg, home of Germany's wonderful smoked beers; and Düsseldorf, where you can stay at the Im Fuschen bed and breakfast. It's attached to one of the great alt breweries and is just a short walk from several other alt breweries.

In Brussels, drop by the Cantillion brewery for a self-guided tour of *lambic*-making at its rustic best. Later, book yourself for dinner at Spinakopka. Many of their dishes are cooked with Belgian beer, and a wide selection of beers is available for tasting.

If you go east to the Czech Republic, be sure to stop in Pilsen for the tour at the Pilsner Urquell brewery. And in Prague, don't miss the wonderful black beer at the U Fleku brewpub.

If London is your destination, be sure to go to the White Horse Pub in Parson's Green—one of the finest real-ale pubs in the world. Brewers Fuller's and Young's are in the same general area of the city, and their tours are quite enjoyable. For a one-night trip out of London, visit Gale's Brewery to the south in a small town called Horndean in Hampshire. You can stay at the brewery's Ship and Bell Hotel. If you're headed north, find the small town of Kimberly in Nottinghamshire, where you can bed down at the Nelson and Railway pub and enjoy great locally brewed beers along with great hospitality.

Quick Carbonation—Not! Like most homebrewers, Bryan hated waiting for weeks for his beer to carbonate in the bottle. Relying on yeast to get the job done tried his patience.

One day at work, he was unpacking a shipment that had been cooled with dry ice. It hit him: dry ice was frozen carbon dioxide! Maybe he could quickly carbonate his beer by adding a cube of dry ice to each bottle instead of priming sugar.

The idea seemed sound. Bryan spent an evening calculating the exact weight of dry ice needed per bottle of beer and determining what size the cube should be. He couldn't wait to try out his idea.

The next weekend, he had a batch of beer ready for bottling. He filled a dozen bottles with beer and set the caps nearby so he could seal the bottles quickly after he added the dry ice. He sliced a dozen dry ice cubes and was ready to go.

BLOOPERS

Bryan dropped a cube into the first bottle and quickly capped it. Things seemed to go well, so he pressed on, filling and capping more bottles. But as he was capping the eighth bottle, he was startled by a loud explosion from the first. Fortunately, he had set the capped bottles inside a wooden beer case, but he was still showered with beer and bits of glass as they descended after hitting the ceiling.

Rather than risk injury from the explosions by trying to open the bottles, Bryan threw a large cutting board on top of the box and abandoned ship until the fireworks were over. Three years later, he was still finding fragments of glass in the nether regions of his kitchen.

On reviewing the situation, Bryan determined his calculations had been correct. The problem, it seems, is that the carbon dioxide was liberated from the dry ice far faster than it could dissolve in the beer. As a result, pressure built up, causing the bottles to explode.

Another brilliant beer-making strategy foiled by the laws of physics!

ADORN YOURSELF WITH BEER

MOST BEER FOLKS ARE READILY willing to admit their *cervisiaphilia,* and often their attire and accessories announce their obsession. One creative extra that several women have added to the mix is earrings. The first innovative pair I saw used small bottle openers as the dangle. This creates a practical solution for those who are always in need of an opener, and it certainly attracted attention from nearby beer-loving men. Other beery items that have become earrings include bottle caps and the little plastic goats that come around the neck of Celebrator *doppelbock* bottles.

Guys are not locked out of this, either. Rings and belt buckles are definite possibilities. Vests and hats offer endless opportunity. I've even seen plastic neck glasses decorated with beery themes that included glued-on kernels of malt and small hop vines complete with fresh green cones! Cook up your own novel beerwear and model it the next time you meet with beery friends.

BEER REPAIR

LIKE MOST HOMEBREWERS, you've grown used to good beer. Suddenly picnics, ball games, and family events take on new meaning. Usually they mean bad beer. You know—thin, flavorless, forgettable stuff that makes you wish you had a beer with some guts to it.

Rather than suffer bad beer or shun social events that mark normal human life, you can do something to improve what you are drinking. Creative beer juggernaut Randy Mosher came up with a potion a few years ago called Beer Repair (copyrights and patents pending, I'm sure). Basically this stuff is just concentrated beer flavor. Malt extract forms the base, and some hop flavor and aroma extracts are thrown in for good measure. Mix them up, package in a small squeeze bottle, and carry to your next bad beer event. When the beer is served, pull out your handy bottle of suds-saver and give your weak-kneed beer a shot in the arm. Guaranteed to improve aroma and flavor! If making the mix is too much trouble, just bring along some malt extract and a bottle of hop flavor extract. It's not as elegant, but just as effective.

DROP-BY-DROP BEER CHRONICLE

EVEN IF YOU DON'T DO YOUR OWN laundry, you've probably noticed that beer can create a terrible stain on clothing. It will also stain walls, floors, rugs, and even postcards. Yes, postcards. What better way to remember a friend or chronicle your own beer experiences than with a beer-splattered postcard?

This idea started as a way to taunt beer-loving friends who missed a great beer-drinking experience. Get a postcard, and drip a drop or two on it every time you try a new beer. Let it dry. Before long, you'll have a wonderful memento of the beers. Label the splotches (if you can remember what they were) and mail the card to the friend who stayed behind. As a log of your own experiences, make a second card and mail it to yourself.

This idea is easy to implement and fun to have for future reference. I've seen it executed on T-shirts and can imagine it on coasters, placemats, business cards, screen savers, mouse pads, posters, and many other paper and cloth items. You might even consider keeping a log like this for every beer you brew—perhaps in a small diary, you could record tasting notes along with the telltale drop.

Who knows? A thousand years from now, an archaeologist might find your records and see them as a treasure trove of turn-of-the-millennium brewing technology.

MAKE YOUR OWN MALT VINEGAR

BEER IS THE STARTING POINT FOR the production of malt vinegar, a classic condiment for English-style fish and chips (fried fish with French fries). In addition, malt vinegar is a versatile cooking ingredient that can be used in salads and sauces of many kinds. In short, it's a great thing to have around—and easy to make, once you have some beer.

Malty beers seem best suited to vinegar-making, although I suppose some folks would like hop flavor in their vinegar, too. Don't use a bad batch of beer to make vinegar, because any off-flavors will survive in the finished product. Just divert a quart or a gallon of beer from a finished batch before it's primed or carbonated. Place the beer in a clean container and add a "mother of vinegar" culture, which you can get from a homebrew or wine shop. After about three months, the alcohol will be completely converted to acetic acid. Bottle the vinegar and save the culture for your next batch of vinegar.

CARROT BEER

THEY SAY GEORGE WASHINGTON, OR maybe it was Thomas Jefferson, made beer using starch from vegetables to help stretch the available barley. Well, carrots may not be the starchiest of veggies, but after hearing of this colonial practice, I've always wanted to make a beer that included them. For better or worse, here it is.

"ORANGE YOU NICE" CARROT BEER (makes 1 gallon)
Original gravity: 1.044
2 pounds carrots, sliced and diced in a food processor (Alternately, cut into 1/8-inch slices before cooking, and then mash the soft carrots afterward.)
1.5 pounds crushed pale ale or Pilsener malt
0.1 ounce 3–4% alpha-acid hops (0.3–0.4 AAU) (I used Cascade)

Place the diced carrots in a pot with 2 gallons of cold water and heat. Boil the carrots 90 minutes. Turn off the heat and let mixture sit 20 to 30 minutes or until it has cooled to between 160 and 165 °F (71 and 74 °C). Mix 1.5 pounds of crushed malt in with the cooked carrots and water. Let stand 1 to 2 hours, stirring occasionally. Next, heat the mixture to a boil and boil 5 minutes. (If you think this is a bit involved, just remember that pioneer life wasn't easy!)

Collect the liquid from this mash using a small lautering device, a large strainer, or a grain bag. Wash the mixture of carrots and grain with hot water after it has drained, and include the runnings in the collected liquid. Bring the resulting wort to a boil for 45 minutes, adding 0.1 ounce (about a teaspoon of pellets) of 3 to 4 percent alpha-acid hops (0.3 to 0.4 AAU) after the first 15 minutes. After the boil, cool and pitch with about half a package of dry ale yeast.

The finished beer is uniquely orange and quite fruity, and it has a unique sweetness from the carrots. Give it a whirl for your next vegetarian dinner!

HOP JELLY

THOUGHT YOU'D HEARD IT ALL? Now here comes hop jelly! Developed by Tom Betchkal of Racine Wisconsin (and spotted by Carol DeBell at Nort's Worts in Kenosha, Wisconsin), it's light green, and I'm told it tastes kind of like pepper jelly. Best of all, you can adjust the hoppiness to suit your own tastes. Here is Tom's recipe:

HOP JELLY
1 1/2–3 cups apple juice
1/2–1 1/2 ounces whole hops, any variety
3 1/2 cups table sugar
2 tablespoons lemon juice
About 3 drops green food coloring
About 1 drop yellow food coloring
One 3-ounce pouch Certo liquid fruit pectin

The first step is to infuse the apple juice with hop flavors.

Bring 1 1/2 cups of apple juice to a simmer. Add the hops, using a hop bag to contain them if available. Simmer the hops in the apple juice for about 5 minutes. Remove and drain the hops, and then strain the apple juice through cheesecloth or a clean hand towel to remove the remaining bits of hop. Add fresh apple juice to bring the total volume of juice up to 1 1/2 cups.

From here on, follow the jelly instructions on the Certo package, adding the remaining ingredients listed above. Makes about 24 ounces of jelly.

When it's finished, spread some on your toast in the morning or combine with cream cheese on Ritz crackers to go with your favorite beer.

ORANGE AMBROSIA MEAD

SOME PEOPLE LIKE MEAD DRY and tart, often sparkling like champagne. Personally, I go more for the sweet and still kind—a sort of after-dinner-liqueur like *chambord*.

Of the dozen or so meads I've made, this is my favorite. Unfortunately, it goes fast, so I've never been able to share it with many other people. I'll just share the recipe so others can make their own supply!

ORANGE AMBROSIA MEAD (makes 1 gallon)
4 pounds orange-blossom honey
1 vanilla bean
1 quart fresh-squeezed orange juice (6 modest-sized oranges)
1 teaspoon yeast nutrient
1/4 ounce weight malic acid
1 tablespoon very strong tea
1 package Epernay 2 yeast

For each gallon of finished mead, heat half a gallon of water to boiling. Turn off fire and add honey, yeast nutrient, malic acid, and tea. Stir until all ingredients are dissolved.

Turn on heat and boil 10 minutes. At the end of this time, turn off the heat and add the orange juice. Let the mixture sit until cool; then transfer it to the fermenter and, if needed, add enough cold water to reach the targeted batch volume. Pitch the yeast and ferment at 60 to 75 °F (15 to 24 °C).

After about a month, rack the mead into a secondary fermenter. Let it ferment at least another month—maybe two or three—before bottling. Bottle without priming for still mead; prime as you would for beer to make sparkling mead.

You can start tasting this wonderful potion about six months after it's brewed, but it will continue to improve with age for a year or two. Give it some time, and you'll be rewarded!

Maribeth "MB" Raines and Steve Casselman—
A Match Made in Maltose

Their first date was at a brewpub; their wedding was at a brewery. Sounds like a brewer's perfect match.

It has been so long since Steve Casselman started brewing, he can't really remember when it was. But by the time Steve and MB met, he was making fifteen-gallon batches, and a friend had just helped him to create two huge propane burners for outdoor brewing. "When he turned those burners on, the flames were so big they would engulf a fifteen-gallon kettle," MB recalls.

PROFILE

One of her first contributions to the household brew equipment came when MB spotted a newspaper ad for an auction. It was to include several stainless-steel vessels suitable for brewing. At the auction site, they also found sixty-gallon pots that were perfect for their monster burners, but unfortunately those weren't for sale. "I kept pestering the auction guy," says Steve, "but he really didn't show any interest in helping us out until I told him we were going to use them for making beer." Four of those sixty-gallon vessels are now the heart of their homebrewing system.

MB learned her brewing from Steve, and Steve got his early lessons from fellow members of the Maltose Falcons homebrew club. Shortly after the two met, the Falcons won the California Homebrew Club of the Year award, and with it a free party at the Anchor Brewery in San Francisco.

"That trip to Anchor was my first introduction to the Falcons," says MB. "And it was also the first weekend trip that Steve and I took together." In the Falcons, she found a group of people that shared her interests and attitudes. "I knew I had found a home," she says.

Six years later, the couple returned to the brewery for the same celebration with the Falcons, and they added a special ceremony of their own. Surrounded by family, friends, and Falcons, they were married in front of the brewery. The guests lighted the ceremony with candles and threw malt instead of rice. Afterward, everyone rejoined the party inside and a long evening of revelry began.

Like most newlyweds, Steve and MB saved their leftover wedding cake, but they didn't wait a year to put it to use. Four or five months after the ceremony, they used the cake in a special commemorative wedding brew.

"Our only big mistake was not taking off the butter icing before we put the cake in the kettle," says Steve. "We spent a lot of time skimming all the fat off the top of the wort before we could continue with the brew." The resulting beer was a very chocolatey imperial stout. It took an award in competition about the time of their anniversary, and kegs of it remained on tap at their house for more than two years.

Even with their overgrown homebrewing setup, the couple remains involved in larger brewing ventures. MB has used her training as a biochemist to design yeast-handling systems for homebrewers and to isolate brewers' yeast strains sold by Brewtek. She is also brewmaster and vice president of production for a contract brewing company that is marketing a *kölsch*-style beer under the name "Hollywood Blonde."

Steve has been active in leading the Maltose Falcons, serving as president several times and on the board for ten years. He also has served on the board of advisors for the American Homebrewers Association for several years.

Both continue to find their enjoyment in brewing from the constant learning. "There is a lot of information out there," says Steve. "If you dig a little, you can find some really interesting things."

GLOSSARY

adjunct. Any unmalted grain or other fermentable ingredient added to the mash.

aeration. The action of introducing air to the wort at various stages of the brewing process.

airlock. See *fermentation lock.*

airspace. See *ullage.*

alcohol by volume (v/v). The percentage of volume of alcohol per volume of beer. To calculate the approximate volumetric alcohol content, subtract the terminal gravity from the original gravity and divide the result by 75. For example: $1.050 - 1.012 = 0.038 / 0.0075 = 5$ percent alcohol by volume.

alcohol by weight (w/v). The percentage weight of alcohol per volume of beer. For example: 3.2 percent alcohol by weight = 3.2 grams of alcohol per 100 centiliters of beer. Alcohol by weight can be converted to alcohol by volume by multiplying by 0.795.

ale. Historically, an unhopped malt beverage. Now a generic term for hopped beers produced by top fermentation, as opposed to lagers, which are produced by bottom fermentation.

all-extract beer. A beer made with only malt extract as opposed to one made from barley, or a combination of malt extract and barley.

all-grain beer. A beer made with only malted barley as opposed to one made from malt extract, or from malt extract and malted barley.

all-malt beer. A beer made with only barley malt with no adjuncts or refined sugars.

alpha acid. A soft resin in hop cones. When boiled, alpha acids are converted to iso-alpha-acids, which account for 60 percent of a beer's bitterness.

alpha-acid unit. A measurement of the potential bitterness of hops that is expressed by the percentage of alpha acid. Low is 2 to 4 percent; medium is 5 to 7 percent; high is 8 to 12 percent. Abbrev: A.A.U.

alt. The german word for old. This is an old-fashioned, top-fermenting style of beer that undergoes a cold lagering for maturation.

attenuation. The reduction in the wort's specific gravity caused by the transformation of sugars into alcohol and carbon dioxide gas.

blow-by (blow-off). A single-stage homebrewing fermentation method in which a plastic tube is fitted into the mouth of a carboy, with the other end submerged in a pail of sterile water. Unwanted residues and carbon dioxide are expelled through the tube, while air is prevented from coming into contact with the fermenting beer, thus avoiding contamination.

carbonation. The process of introducing carbon dioxide gas into a liquid by: (1) injecting the finished beer with carbon dioxide; (2) adding young fermenting beer to finished beer for a renewed fermentation (kraeusening); (3) priming (adding sugar) to fermented wort prior to bottling, creating a secondary fermentation in the bottle; or (4) finishing fermentation under pressure.

carboy. A large glass, plastic, or earthenware bottle.

chill haze. Haziness caused by protein and tannin during the secondary fermentation.

dry hopping. The addition of hops to the primary fermenter, the secondary fermenter, or to casked beer to add aroma and hop character to the finished beer without adding significant bitterness.

dry malt. Malt extract in powdered form.

EBC (European Brewery Convention). See *SRM*.

fermentation lock. A one-way valve, which allows carbon dioxide gas to escape from the fermenter while excluding contaminants.

final specific gravity. The specific gravity of a beer when fermentation is complete.

fining. The process of adding clarifying agents to beer during secondary fermentation to precipitate suspended matter.

hop pellets. Finely powdered hop cones compressed into tablets. Hop pellets are 20 to 30 percent more bitter by weight than the same variety in loose form.

hydrometer. A glass instrument used to measure the specific gravity of liquids as compared to water, consisting of a graduated stem resting on a weighted float.

International Bitterness Unit. This is an empirical quantity, which was originally designed to measure the concentration of iso-alpha-acids in milligrams per liter (parts per million). Most procedures will also measure a small amount of uncharacterized soft resins, so IBUs are generally 5 to 10 percent higher than iso-alpha acid concentrations.

isinglass. A gelatinous substance made from the swim bladder of certain fish and added to beer as a fining agent.

kraeusen. *n.* The rocky head of foam which appears on the surface of the wort during fermentation. *v.* To add fermenting wort to fermented beer to induce carbonation through a secondary fermentation.

lager. *n.* A generic term for any bottom-fermented beer. Lager brewing is presently the predominant brewing method worldwide except in Britain, where top-fermented ales dominate. *v.* To store beer at near-zero temperatures in order to precipitate yeast cells and proteins and improve taste.

lauter tun. A vessel in which the mash settles and the grains are removed from the sweet wort through a straining process. It has a false, slotted bottom and spigot.

malt. Barley that has been steeped in water, germinated, then dried in kilns. This process converts insoluble starchs to soluble substances and sugars.

malt extract. A thick syrup or dry powder prepared from malt.

mashing. Mixing ground malt with water to extract the fermentables, degrade haze-forming proteins, and convert grain starches to fermentable sugars and also nonfermentable carbohydrates.

modification. The physical and chemical changes in barley as a result of malting, or the degree to which these changes have occured, as determined by the growth of the acrospire.

original gravity. The specific gravity of wort previous to fermentation. A measure of the total amount of dissolved solids in wort.

pH. A measure of acidity or alkalinity of a solution, usually on a scale of one to fourteen, where seven is neutral.

primary fermentation. The first stage of fermentation, during which most fermentable sugars are converted to ethyl alcohol and carbon dioxide.

priming sugar. A small amount of corn, malt, or cane sugar added to bulk beer prior to racking or at bottling to induce a new fermentation and create carbonation.

racking. The process of transferring beer from one container to another, especially into the final package (bottles, kegs, etc.).

secondary fermentation. The second, slower stage of fermentation, lasting from a few weeks to many months depending on the type of beer, or a fermentation occuring in bottles or casks and initiated by priming or by adding yeast.

sparging. Spraying the spent grains in the mash with hot water to retrieve the remaining malt sugar.

specific gravity. A measure of a substance's density as compared to that of water, which is given the value of 1.000 at 39.2 °F (4 °C). Specific gravity has no accompanying units, because it is expressed as a ratio.

SRM (Standard Reference Method) and EBC (European Brewery Convention). Two different analytical methods of describing color developed by comparing color samples. Degrees SRM, approximately equivalent to degrees Lovibond, are used by the American Society of Brewing Chemists while degrees EBC are European units. The following equations show approximate conversions:

$$(°EBC) = 2.65 \times (°Lovibond) - 1.2$$
$$(°Lovibond) = 0.377 \times (°EBC) + 0.45$$

starter. A batch of fermenting yeast, added to the wort to initiate fermentation.

strike temperature. The initial temperature of the water when the malted barley is added to it to create the mash.

tannin. See *polyphenol*.

trub. Suspended particles resulting from the precipitation of proteins, hop oils, and tannins during boiling and cooling stages of brewing.

ullage. The empty space between a liquid and the top of its container. Also called airspace or headspace.

vorlauf. To recirculate the wort from the mash tun back through the grain bed to clarify.

v/v. See *alcohol by volume*.

w/v. See *alcohol by weight*.

water hardness. The degree of dissolved minerals in water.

wort. The mixture that results from mashing the malt and boiling the hops, before it is fermented into beer.

REFERENCES

Loysen, Tracy, ed. 1990. *Beer and Brewing,* vol. 7. Boulder, CO: Brewers Publications.
Renfrow, Cindy. 1994. *A Sip through Time.* Pownal, VT: Storey Publishing.
Zymurgy 15, no. 3 (Fall 1992): 7.

INDEX

accessories, beer-themed, 164

acetic acid (vinegar), 78, 167

acid blend, 23

activities for groups. *See* group activities

aeration of wort, 115

aging: beer, 117, 130, 135; hard cider, 21; lambics, 79; meads, 24, 172; strong ales, 138; in wood, 90

agitation, 130

Alaskan Brewing Company, 147

ale, 66–67, 140. *See also* spiced beers

all-grain brewing, 5, 6, 15

alpha-acid content, 98, 118, 119–20. *See also* hops

American Homebrewers Association, 39, 48, 110, 141, 173

apparent attenuation, 68

apple juice, 20, 152

Artz, Dot, 133–34

Artz, Tim, 133–34

Ashworth, Judy, 70

Association of Brewers, 101, 110

attemperation coils, 132

attenuation, apparent, 68

backpack, 114

bacteria, 54, 107. *See also* infection; lambics

Bamburg, 161

bappir beer, 153–55

barley wine (recipe), 138–39

barley, 9, 104, 126; roasted, 84; in wheat beer, 13–14. *See also* malts

base malt, 64

beer cocktails, 70–71

beer identification, 35

Beer Judge Certification Program, 30

beer repair potion, 165

beer styles, 58, 101

beers: ancient, 153; Belgian, 133–34 (*See also* lambics); blending, 70–71; commercial, 82; as food, 149; improving bad, 165; naming, 96; transporting, 114, 116

Belgium, 78, 79, 161

Bell, Larry, 126

berries, 73

Betchkal, Tom, 170

births, celebrating, 117

bitterness, 119–20

black and tan [cocktail], 70

blending beers, 70–71, 135

blowoff tubes, 8

bock beers, 71; malts for, 18

boiling, 12

bottle color, 49

bread, 151; *bappir* (recipe), 153–54; beer-making from, 153–55; caramel malt (recipe), 28; malt extract (recipe), 31

Breakfast Cereal Brewoff, 22

Brettanomyces bruxellensis, 79

Brettanomyces lambicus, 79

brew-a-thons, 106

brewery tours, 161

brewing calendar, 58

brewing: commercial, 59, 123; equipment setup, 122–23 (*See also* equipment making); organisms involved, 78–79; outdoor, 102–3; places for, 39–40, 102–3. *See also* homebrewing

brewoffs, 22, 48

brewpubs, 59, 75, 109

Brewtown Brewmasters, 9

brezen, 36, 136

bride ale, 156–57

brown ales, malts for, 18

brunch, 36

Brussels, 162

BURP (Brewers United for Real Potables) homebrew club, 133

caramelization, 111

carbonation: in bottle, 162–63; cider, 21; kvass, 26; mead, 24; real ale, 140; root beer, 41

carboys, cleaning, 92

cardamom, 53

carrot beer (recipe), 168–69

cask ale, 140

casks, 90

Casselman, Steve, 172–73

cereals, breakfast, 22

cheese, 151

cheesecake, smoked porter (recipe), 147–48

Chicago Beer Society (CBS), 2, 22, 48, 96, 101, 102, 141

chicken: marinated (recipe), 53; wort-crusted (recipe), 129

chili, 145

chili pepper beers, 93

chilling: beer, 86–87; wort, 132

Christmas beers, 66

cider, hard, 20–21

citric acid, 25

clarity, 56

cock ale, 72

cocktails, 70

coffee, 33

cold plates, 86–87

color: of beer, 69, 88–89, 111, 117; of bottle, 49

cookies, spent grain (recipe), 32

copper ales, malts for, 18

copper tubing, 86

coriander, 53

corn, 107, 112

corn syrup, 42

Correnty, Paul, 21

Craft Brewing Association (England), 130

craft-beer business, 59

cream ale, 70

Crystal/caramel malts, 5, 7–8, 28, 37. *See also* malts
Curaçao orange peel, 53
Czech Republic, 162

dark beers, 158
Davis, Brian, 1
Dean, Ray, 93
DeBell, Carol, 170
degrees SRM, 88
dispensers, 114, 121
distillation, 107
doppelbock, 66
double beers, 80, 81
dry hopping, with chilies, 93
dry ice, 162–63
dunkelweizen, 37
Düsseldorf, 161

earrings, 164
education, 30, 173; on beer styles, 35, 38; brewers, 61, 62; homebrew hotline, 150; judges, 61; publicity and, 39–40; style meetings, 101. *See also* group activities
endosperm, 65
equipment making, 16–17, 51; aeration system, 115; cooling coil, 86–87; dispensers, 114, 121–22; fermenter cooling systems, 57; keg cozy, 116; lauter tun/masher, 15

Europe, beer tour of, 161–62
experimentation, 45, 50, 59–60, 103, 119, 173; aging, 90–91; bizarre ingredients, 110, 126, 127
experts, 35. *See also* judging
extract brewing, 6. *See also* malt extract
extracts: malt (*see* malt extract); root beer, 41; spruce, 158; in wheat beer, 13

fats, 72, 173
fermentation: apple juice, 20; mead, 24; products of, 78; secondary, 56; speed, 68; temperature, 57, 132–33
fermenters, 8, 45, 90
fetters, 130
filtration, 56
final gravity, 68
finings, 56, 140
Finland, 9
firkins, 140
flavor faults, 49, 54
flavors: adding, 156; beer, 165; fruity, 80, 81; relationship to color, 111; smoky, 43–44, 63; spruce, 158; from wood, 90
fluid flow, 143
food, 95; for beer tastings, 151
fruit beers, 73–74
fruit ciders, 133

Gerdemann, Gary, 1
Germany, 161

glass color, 49

glass holster, 12

glasses, 11–12, 56

grain mites, 148–49

grains: in commercial beers, 112; fresh-roasted, 18; specialty, 7; spent, 32. *See also* malts

grains of paradise, 53

gravity: aging and, 135; apple juice, 20; bitterness calculation and, 120; final, 68; original, 68; specific, 68–69; X designations, 138

Great Northern Brewers Club, 106

grist, 112

group activities, 2–3, 39–40, 141. *See also* judging; tastings; beer name creation, 96–97; brew-a-thons, 106; brew-chef dinners, 95; brewoffs, 22, 48; color readings, 89; eccentric brewing, 126; homebrew expo, 141–42; identification testings, 35; style meetings, 101; win-a-trip party, 128

haze, 56

hefe, 37

helles, 74

homebrew clubs, 150

homebrew expo, 141–42

homebrewing: assistance hotline, 150; novices, 106

honey, 24, 76–77, 124; types, 125

hop devil, 100

hop festival, 100

hop jelly (recipe), 170

hops, 34; alpha-acid content, 98; aroma, 98; in coffee, 33; drying, 91, 99; extracting bitterness, 12; flavor, 5; growing, 98–99; in pale ale, 131; utilization values, 120

Hordeum vulgare. *See* barley

Horndean (England), 162

hydrometers, 69

IBU. *See* international bitterness units

ice cream, 160

India pale ale, 130–31

infection, 54, 78, 130

international bitterness units, 119–20

Jackson, Michael, 22, 35

Jones, Greg, 109

judging, 61, 62. *See also* experts; tastings

June-Bug Bride Ale (recipe), 157

juniper, 9

Katz, Solomon, 153

keg cozy, 116

kegs: sanitizing, 19; soda, 86, 114, 116; tapping, 140

Kentucky Common Beer (recipe), 108–9

Kimberly (England), 162

Klopfer, Gary, 16–17

Klopfer, Tom, 16–17
Korzonas, Al, 22
kristal, 37
kvass, 25–26

labels, 156
lactic acid, 78, 107
lagers, 133; malts for, 18; Miller's Envy,
    112–13
lambics, 70, 73, 78–79, 134
Lambswool (recipe), 152
lauter tuns, 15, 132
lautering, 15, 143; kvass, 26
light, effect on beer, 49–50, 102
London, 162
Lovibond rating system, 7, 8

mace, 72
magazines, 75
Majority Ale, 117
malt extract, 5; in bread, 31; in ice cream,
    160; in meat marinade, 53; test brew-
    ings with, 68–69
malt vinegar, 167
malted milk shake, 27
malting, 104, 112
malto-dextrin, 42
Maltose Falcons homebrew club, 122, 172
malts, 104–5; color, 18, 44; Crystal/caramel,
    5, 7–8, 28; dark, 111; drying, 18, 43;
    flavors, 69; modification, 65, 105; pale

ale, 18; roasting/toasting, 18, 43;
    smoking, 43–44, 145; specialty, 7;
    tasting, 7–8, 64–65; two-row, 18; in
    waffles, 52. *See also* grains; malt
    extract
maltsters, 7, 64, 104
marinade (meat), 53
marriage, 156–57, 172–73
mashing, 15–16, 45, 143; mixed-grain, 112
maturation, 135; time, 58, 66
Maytag, Fritz, 153
McCrorie, James, 130
meads, 23–24, 124, 133; orange ambrosia
    (recipe), 171–72
meat, 53, 72, 129
media, 39, 40
melanoidins, 117
milk, malted, 27
Miller's Envy (recipe), 112–13
mit-hefe, 37
Mosher, Randy, 11–12, 50–51, 96, 114, 146,
    165
mother of vinegar culture, 167
Munich, 161
must, 24

naming beers, 96
National Homebrew Competition, 123
National Homebrewers' Conference, 11, 48,
    108
National Homebrew Day, 39

National Saké Center, 62
neck glasses, 11
newsletters, 141
Norris, Tim, 11, 48
Now Here's the Pitch (recipe), 159

old ale, 135
"Orange You Nice" Carrot Beer (recipe), 168–69
original gravity, 68
outdoor brewing, 102–3
Owens, Bill, 74–75
oxidation, 90
oxygenator systems, 115

pale ales, 71, 101; malts for, 18
Papazian, Charlie, 35
Parker, Jim, 109–10
pasteurizing honey, 76–77
Pediococcus damnosus, 79
Pilsen, 162
Pilseners, 101
pitching, 68
porters, 43, 70, 84, 101; malts for, 18; recipe, 85; smoked, 147
potions, 146
poultry, cooking in wort, 129
Prague, 162
pretzels, 36; recipe, 136–37
proteins, 72; coagulating, 12; hazing from, 56
Pumpkin Beer (recipe), 5–6

raffle, 142
Rahn, Phil, 59
Raines, Maribeth "MB", 172–73
raisins, 72
Rastetter, Tim, 12
rauchbier, 43
real ale, 140
recipe formulation, 119
record-keeping, 91, 117, 127; honey varieties, 124; with stains, 166; time capsule, 144
refrigeration, 57. *See also* chilling
Reinheitsgebot, 56
rice, 112
rice hulls, 143
Richman, Darryl, 122–23
rocks, 59–60, 63
root beer, 41–42
rye, 9, 10, 25, 107

sahti, 9–10
sanitizing, 19, 54; aeration stone, 115; honey, 76; testing, 54–55; wood chips, 90
sausage, 36
Schaefer, Mike, 9
Score Plus One Ale (recipe), 117–18
scotches, 90
settling, 56
silica gel, 56
siphoning, 155
Six-Pack Club, 38
skunkiness, 49–50, 102–3

Skypeck, Chuck, 59, 63
sleep, hop-induced, 34
Slosberg, Pete, 29–30
smoked beers, 71, 91
snow, 44
soda kegs, 86, 114, 116
sour mash beers, 107–9
Southern California Homebrew Festival, 121
Spangler, Ray, 107
sparging, 26
specific gravity, 69
spiced beers, 72, 94; potions for, 146; spice proportions, 146; spiced ale (recipe), 66–67
spices, 53, 94, 146
spigots, 15
spiles, 140
spruce beer, 158–59
SRM. *See* Standard Reference Method
stainless steel, 19, 90
stains, 166
Standard Reference Method (SRM), 88
starch (in malt), 104–5
steel, stainless, 19, 90
sterilization, 54–55. *See also* sanitizing
stewing, 7
stone beers, 59–60, 63
storage, 117–18, 135. *See also* aging; malts, 148–49; pale ale, 130
stouts, 43, 74, 84, 101; malts for, 18; recipe, 84–85; Russian imperial, 117

straining, 155
strength of beer, 126
strong ales, 138–39
style meetings, 101
sugars: in hard cider, 20; in root beer, 41. *See also* honey
supplies, 122; safeguarding, 148–49

tannin, 23
tapping kegs, 140
tastings, 35, 38, 61, 62, 101; food for, 151; honey, 124; malts, 7–8, 64–65; matching exercise, 62; porters versus stouts, 84. *See also* judging
temperature, 57; of fermentation, 132–33; serving, 86, 116
test batches, 45, 68–69
time capsule, 144
Trappist beers, 80–81
travel, 161–62
triple beers, 80, 81

van Schaik, Jan, 44
Vanilla Malt Freeze (recipe), 160
vegetable starches, 168
vinegar, 78; malt, 167
vodka, 146
Vulgare Day, 126

waffles, 52
water: outflow, 92; quality, 44, 46; source, 102

weiss, 37

weisse, 37

weisswurst, 36

weizen, 13, 36–37; recipe, 14; rye, 143

weizenbock, 37, 66

wheat beers, 13–14, 36–37

wheat wine, 143

wheat, 107

whiskey, 107

Whitbread ale yeast, 21, 47

wit beer, 53

wood, 90–91

wort, 46; aeration of, 115; gravity, 20; sanitizing, 12; sterile, 82–83

wort chillers, 132

yeast starters, 45, 68, 82–83

yeasts, 46; in hard cider, 20; harvesting, 82;
hazing from, 56; for mead, 23; for pale
ale, 47; storing samples of, 73; for
Trappist-style beer, 80–81; varieties,
82–83; for wheat beers, 13, 37, 47;
wild, 78